A HISTORY
OF ENGLISH COSTUME

A History of

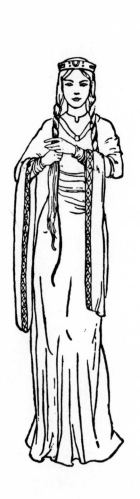

English Costume

Written and illustrated by

IRIS BROOKE

Theatre Arts Books

NEW YORK

TO MY MOTHER

Copyright © 1972 by Iris Brooke

Library of Congress Catalog Card Number: 72-85476

ISBN 0-87830-056-2

Published by Theatre Arts Books
333 Sixth Avenue/New York 10014

Printed in Great Britain

INTRODUCTION

When this book was first published there were very few costume books available but it was my intention to write a sort of skeleton guide to whatever other publications existed at that time. I believe that in its revised state it can still serve the same purpose although there are today dozens of books dealing with Fashion and Costume containing beautiful reproductions of paintings from the brushes of some of the greatest painters in history.

However, it is the ever changing silhouette that really matters if we are to be interested in the fashions of our ancestors and so often the tiny sketches in a landscape yield more information than a portrait where the sitter hopes to impress posterity rather than be seen for the man he is.

In the following pages my intention is still to give an idea of the costumes that might have been worn in England from the Norman Conquest to the present day. While we know that the excesses of the Italian Renaissance did not ever reach the English shores – neither did the strange undress of the ladies depicted in the Bible of Wenceslas IV nor the farthingales worn in Spain in 1460 – we do know that from the fourteenth century onwards strange costumes appeared from other countries and were adopted by the wealthy and fashion conscious. It is useless to imagine that the countries with whom England was allied through royal marriages did not influence the fashions of those who were in any way connected with the courts of Europe even at a very early date. It is thus that we hear of the Flaundrish beaver hat worn by the merchant in Chaucer's *Canterbury*

Tales and of countless other references to 'outlandish' costume from writers through the ensuing centuries.

That simple, useful clothes have always been worn by those people whose lives demanded utility rather than fashion is undeniable. The full, ankle-length petticoats, fitted bodice and varying types of washable headcoverings have been almost timeless whilst the 'slops' or breeches, shirts and some kind of coat or cloak have been men's choice of working attire since time immemorial. That such people had Sunday clothes cut in the fashion of their more prosperous neighbours is equally true, and every crowded scene, depicted by any artist from the Middle Ages till today, shows just how much the contemporary scene was affected by the fashions of that time.

Obviously the more ostentatious fashions were rarely imitated by the poor, though, quite early in England's history, examples are given of extravagances in clothes by those who could ill afford such luxuries.

Chaucer tells us that the Haberdasher, Carpenter, Webber, Dyer and Tapicer were all well dressed. . . . 'Full fresh and new their gear y-trimmed was . . .' and that the Ploughman wore a round coat, the houpelande of the fifteenth century.

To the best of my ability I have endeavoured to omit the majority of the contemporary names for certain garments, because the whole problem of naming and renaming them as they change their shapes and uses would become far too obscure for the general reader to follow. Indeed each garment (unless of foreign origin with its original name being retained) has been adapted by a new generation, changed and adopted for their own uses or needs, perhaps renamed – or given a new foreign name – to make some contemporary difference obvious, and eventually altered entirely from what it was in its conceived form. Any reader who wants to proceed further into the labyrinths of descriptive costume language should consult a costume dictionary or encyclopedia; possibly a different one for each century, for there is much nonsense in Planche's publication of 1876 – though a very great deal of scholarly work.

A different language exists in every century, and every country is responsible for new inventions; a petticoat for instance begins as a little coat, turns into a skirt, then an undergarment. A kirtle changes into a gown, a bonnet from a hat becomes a coif or a linen head-covering and eventually the nonsensical little 'postage stamp with a couple of bootlaces attached' of the late nineteenth century.

A thousand changes take place as the fashions alter and no vocabulary can keep up with the latest names any more than we can be completely *au fait* with the new colour ranges which decorate the labels of nail varnishes or lipsticks.

Comfort has never been a primary consideration in the vagaries of fashions. In fact, more often than not the most improbable and absurd ideas have been taken quite seriously by a new generation just because they appear strange and perhaps uncouth. We do not progress in the sense of practicability but only in the sense of perpetual change, which is no advancement.

Nevertheless costume is important because it is custom, and custom and habit have helped to shape our history just as much as political manœuvrings and geographical discoveries.

This little volume, therefore, can be regarded only as a fair guide through the jungles of clouts and finery which were the daily habits of our ancestors.

IRIS BROOKE 1972

ILLUSTRATIONS

CONTENTS

Chapter 1

WILLIAM THE CONQUEROR
TO EDWARD III—1066 to 1327

At the time of the Norman Conquest simplicity of cut which amounted almost to a uniform prevailed. The standard lines of a tunic were based on Fig. 1, the only variations being in length and width. The sleeves were, without exception, tight-fitting, and several inches longer than the arm, worn pushed back in a series of concertina-like folds often from wrist to biceps. Sometimes the tunic was split at the sides and almost always finished with a band of embroidery, the richness of design governed only by the financial status of the wearer, the originality by the artistic inclinations of his female relations.

The other more important items of clothing were the 'braies' and 'hose'. The 'braies' were cut on similar lines to a pyjama-trouser, slightly closer at the ankle, and made of linen. They were in general use in England when this history begins. Sometimes they were bound with cross-gartering but, more often, worn with the short hose reaching from ankle to knee. During the last years of the eleventh century the 'braies' were shortened and the 'hose' lengthened. The latter then reached well up the thigh and were tied to the belt at the sides, whilst the 'braies' were either cut closer, more like tights, or else shortened to the knee, in which case they were usually worn outside the tunic, thus achieving the importance of an outer garment.

The 'hose' had no foot, unless they happened to be made of leather or felt when they resembled a tight-fitting boot, occasionally embroidered at the top. More often the shoes, which were made of very flexible leather, were worn over the bare foot.

These shoes were cut high at the instep and fastened either at the side or in front. By the end of the century they had acquired an

Fig. 1. – Late Eleventh Century

added few inches at the ankle and were worn rolled or turned down like a cuff.

About the only type of headdress in use during the eleventh century, apart from the hood, was the 'Phrygian Cap' (see Figs 1 and 3). The latter was usually finished with a close-fitting band round the head and a pointed crown. The point curled forward.

Add to these already mentioned garments an undershirt, or

Fig. 2. – 1150

'sherte', made of linen, another tunic with shorter loose-fitting sleeves, a semi-circular cloak, and you have the complete outfit worn in all weather and for all occasions by the Norman and Anglo-Saxon men.

The tunic could be worn in a number of ways and might vary in length from knee to ankle; the supertunic, when worn, was nearly always several inches shorter than the one beneath. (An exception may be seen in Fig. 4.) Often its sides were tucked into the belt, but sometimes the material at the hips was just dragged back and pinned at the sides, giving the draped effect so mannered in contemporary drawings.

Practically all garments were cut on the cross at this period, thus giving the necessary fullness with a minimum of bulk. This theme might be said to govern the cut of clothes throughout the Middle Ages. There are, certainly, exceptions, but the straight-cut, bulky garments were not used to any extent until the time of the Tudors.

Fig. 3. – Late Eleventh Century   *Fig. 4. – 1170*

The somewhat shapeless draperies worn by women consisted of a linen garment and a robe or gown, usually made of wool, and cut on the same lines as the tunics of the male. Sometimes these were supplemented by a third garment, shorter and fuller, and tied at the waist by a girdle or band of embroidery.

The head was never uncovered, except in the cases of very young girls and slaves, until the twelfth century. Sometimes the covering consisted of a small veil worn over the head and shoulders but, more often, it was similar to a large scarf, draped over the head, with the ends crossed under the chin and thrown back over the shoulders. Spot patterns and bands of embroidery were universally used in decorating the garments of both sexes.

Fig. 5. – Late Eleventh Century

The most spectacular changes in the twelfth century took place in the attire of the women. Previously, for hundreds of years, the female figure had been swathed in copious draperies from head to foot, showing nothing of the figure and little of the head and face. Now, towards the middle of the twelfth century, some time between 1120 and 1140, the hair once more becomes a woman's 'crowning glory', so much so that all sorts of schemes and devices were employed to make it appear more abundant and brilliant than nature had originally intended. Cases of silk and gold and silver sheaths were attached to the ends of the plaits to give them additional length.

Fig. 6. – 1160

False hair was mingled with too-scanty locks, and the fashion of binding with ribbons was an easy way to attach an extra few inches to each plait. Two or four plaits were equally prevalent. Sometimes the hair was not twisted but divided into two sections and a ribbon laced between. The parting was always in the centre. Ladies who wished to appear more blonde than they actually were suffered agonies from bleaching, spreading their locks in the strongest sunlight in an endeavour to attain a lighter shade; some years later saffron dye was used for the same purpose. Possibly gentlemen preferred blondes even in the twelfth century!

Little coronets, headbands, or 'fillets' were worn, and sometimes a diminutive veil, but for fifty years or more the hair was not hidden, as it was the most important factor in a fashionable woman's ensemble.

Fig. 7. – Mid-twelfth Century

At about the same time dresses assumed a more figure-fitting style, they were often drawn so tight about the body that a series of rucks appear, reaching from breast to hips (Fig. 6). It is more than probable that some form of corset was worn as early as the twelfth century, most certainly tight-lacing was prevalent in the gowns themselves. It seems probable that the waist was emphasized by binding with a wide strip of linen, wound round and round – some of the contemporary effigies certainly give this impression. The earliest boned and elaborately shaped corset is to be found in the contemporary manuscripts of the latter half of the thirteenth century.

Other excesses of the twelfth century were the absurd lengthening of the sleeves. Either they were cut in a gigantic bell shape with the inside lengthened, or else a cuff was added, this being composed of a band several inches in width and several feet in length, so long in fact that, in order to facilitate movement, they were tied in a gigantic knot – sometimes, even the knot dragged on the ground.

Long girdles, knotted and ornamented with jewels and tassels, took the place of the hitherto unseen belt. The cloak also, when worn, was pushed back so that it barely covered the shoulders and revealed as far as possible the wearer's dress; the one brooch or pin which had served as a fastening gave place to two buttons or

Fig. 8. – 1180

brooches and a cord or ribbon between, stretching across the throat (see Fig. 8).

With their newly gained freedom from all-enveloping convention, women vied with each other to reveal their physical attractions – competitive fashion had arrived.

The waisted, figure-fitting gowns, however, barely lasted in popularity for fifty years; before the close of the twelfth century, women had returned once more to loosely hanging garments, excessively full but belted, and for the most part wore their hair tucked away – not beneath an all-enveloping veil but with the plaits rolled up, either over the ears in shells, or doubled across the nape of the neck and held in place by a loosely meshed net, or linen bag, called a 'crespin'. This net was composed of a variety of materials, from the gold mesh, studded richly with jewels, worn by the wealthy, to the plain, loosely woven woollen ones adopted by the poorer classes.

Eleanor, wife of Henry II, started the vogue for the 'barbette', a band of plain linen worn under the chin and fastened on top of the head; this was frequently worn in conjunction with the 'crespin'

Fig. 9. – 1240

and 'fillet', or headband, and continued in general use until well into the fourteenth century (see Figs 9 and 10).

Little dainty veils of transparent material, decorated with spot patterns and embroidered edges, were worn again; these were cut

Fig. 10. – 1260

on the half-circle, like the cloaks, with the straight edge across the forehead and the back falling in folds to the shoulders.

Throughout the twelfth century men contented themselves with a mere elaboration of the standard schemes. Further embroideries decorated the tunics and super-tunics, richer material and more elaborate colours were the vogue. Collars were deeper and more complicated in design and appear, in many cases, to be entirely separate from the tunic, and made of some metal ornamented with semi-precious stones; there is a rather curious hinged effect in contemporary illustrations which could not have been obtained with the stiffest of embroideries. Gilded leather was, in all probability, also employed for collars and cuffs.

There were a few variations in the matter of headdress; versions and parodies of the original Phrygian cap were manifold, and, with

Fig. 11. – 1250

the exception of the peasant hat, shady and utilitarian, they were practically all brimless and finished with a point on the top.

The tendency towards points was general near the close of the century, especially in the case of hats, hoods and shoes, as these might be elongated to suit the inclinations of the individual.

Fig. 12. – 1180

Apart from the already-mentioned extravagances of the wealthy there was little change, except in the manner of hairdressing. During the opening years of this book the hair had been worn either short or cut to the lobe of the ear but, during the twelfth century, the man of fashion wore his hair long and curled in a variety of ways (see Figs 7 and 13). Sometimes a fringe was cut and rows of curls stuck down to the forehead, all turned inwards towards the centre parting. Often the hair was curled in a series of elongated rolls over the ears and the back hair left untouched; corkscrew ringlets were popular.

Beards also demanded a maximum of attention; these were combed and curled, clipped and parted, and received a grooming which almost rivalled that of the Assyrians in a bygone age.

The thirteenth century shows several innovations and additions to

Fig. 13. – Late Twelfth Century

the garments of the preceding century, most of which apply to both sexes.

The origin of the 'surcote', or sleeveless tunic, can be traced to the 'tabards' and super-tunics worn by the first Crusaders over the 'hauberk'. Obviously some garment was necessary to protect the mail; the sun would have rendered the metal unbearable were it not covered in some way. Sometimes the covering consisted of a tunic with full sleeves, but a sleeveless garment gave more freedom and the simple strip of material, with just a hole for the head and falling to the knees, was the obvious solution to the problem. The civil adaptation of the 'surcote' gave much the same effect, excepting that it was usually joined at the sides from waist to hem. Possibly it became so popular because it had a smaller surface to decorate and because the sleeves and skirts of the tunic underneath made a pleasant contrast (Fig. 14).

Fig. 14. – Mid-thirteenth Century

Another fashion which found its inspiration in the 'surcote' was that shown in Fig. 16 B and C; a sleeved gown, split from waist to armpit. The sleeves could be worn or, if for some reason they were inconvenient, the arms could be slipped through the apertures, leaving the sleeves hanging down the back.

An outer garment which took the place of a cloak is illustrated in Fig. 15. The sleeve was cut like the sleeve of a Japanese kimono, with the split for the hand at the side. Hoods were usually attached and, sometimes, a deep fur collar. These were invariably lined, as were the cloaks, with fur or some contrasting material.

Yet another important change was the very loose arm-hole. Where

Fig. 15. – 1260

the sleeve joined the garment the width was so great that the under-arm seam often commenced at the waist and tapered, in a V shape, to the wrist. This new-shaped sleeve was often worn in conjunction with the 'surcote', the width filling the splits at the sides and giving the effect of a tunic with sleeves of a different colour (see Fig. 14).

As will be seen from one or two examples in this chapter, the 'braies' were worn full and tucked into the hose, thus resembling shortened plus-fours.

The fad for long hair came to an end at the end of the twelfth century. Apart from the fact that it now received a little more grooming and general attention, the hair was again worn as it had been during the latter part of the eleventh century.

Fig. 16. – 1260

Little bonnet-shaped caps called 'coifs' were almost as popular with the men as the 'barbette' was with the women. These came into being at the beginning of the century and, possibly, also found their inspiration in the dress of the Crusaders, who always wore a 'coif' beneath a chain-mail head-covering. The fashion spread and all manner of hats were worn over the 'coif'; in particular, it was a style adopted by sportsmen and soldiers as it was extremely useful in keeping the face free from straying locks of hair.

One or two little alterations will be noticed in the cut of the tunics. Frequently they were split in front and at the sides from hem to waist, and the neck-openings, which for so long had been in front, may occasionally be seen at the side (Fig. 16 A). Panels of decoration were worn down the front of the tunic, from neck to waist – or, more often, from neck to hem. The fashion for hitching the sides

Fig. 18. – 1300

Fig. 17. – Late Thirteenth Century

of the tunic and forming U-shaped folds across the front entirely disappeared about the middle of the century. By the end of the century the tunic had assumed a figure-fitting tightness to the hips.

About 1260 another vogue for long plaits seems to have started, but it received little following as the 'crespin', 'barbette' and 'fillet' continued in popularity. An interesting development of the 'fillet' took place in the form of a curious little pillbox-shaped hat. This was flat-topped and about four inches deep. The edge was frilled, pleated or cut in a series of waves. Crowns were worn over these by the ladies of rank.

Fig. 19. – 1300   Fig. 20. – 1320

It is very difficult to see the difference between the deep 'fillet' and the cap in contemporary illustrations; there are, however, several effigies still in existence which show examples of both.

During the 70's, simplicity was in general favour. The girdle or belt worn by women disappeared and the gown hung in deep folds from shoulder to hem. Sleeves once more became tight-fitting and the hanging cuff, which had been creeping back into fashion, vanished again.

Materials were rich and costly, but the craze for bands of trimming was definitely on the wane.

Fig. 21. – Late Eleventh- and Early Twelfth-Century Designs

Chapter 2

EDWARD III TO HENRY VII— 1327 to 1485

It is during the reign of Edward III (1327–77), that great steps in the advancement of clothes as a decorative medium and an expression of personal taste are found. The perfect fusion of conquerors and conquered had just reached its ultimate end in establishing an English people, speaking English, and with individual tastes which sought expression in outward visible signs.

It is necessary, at this point in the progression of fashion, to give some sort of directory of various names applied to the clothes of the period. So far we have been somewhat limited in this respect.

Firstly, let us take the apparel of the fourteenth-century man : a shirt which varied little, if at all, from its predecessor of the tenth century – definitely an under-garment and rarely to be seen. Over this a 'gipon', which was later alluded to as a doublet. Then came a tunic reaching to the knees, the skirts flared, the sleeves and body closely fitting, and over this a 'cote hardie', 'surcote' or 'surcoat' – cut on somewhat looser lines than the 'gipon' and with loosely hanging sleeves. The 'hose' were like a woman's stocking of the present day and were tied to the waist with strings.

The hood was generally worn and was the typical feature of male costume throughout the fourteenth and fifteenth centuries. Its evolution can be traced step by step in the following pages; at the beginning of the fourteenth century it was merely a cowl with a 'gorget' over the shoulders – a protection for the ears, neck, and shoulders. Gradually the point became elongated and, later, a pipe of the same material, several feet in length, was attached to the point and called

Fig. 22. — 1336

a 'liripipe'. The edge of the 'gorget', following the mode of the time, was 'dagged' — cut in a series of points — thus giving the effect of an ornamental collar. (See Fig. 23 C.)

About 1325 the aperture, which had been originally left for the face, was placed over the head. The ornamental edge of the 'gorget', therefore, hung in folds down one side of the face or stood up like a cockscomb and the 'liripipe' hung down the other side — the latter was then wound round the head, giving a turban-like effect. This fashion lasted for over a hundred years and could be worn as a hood or as a hat. Later the same theme, though lacking its original uses, was enlarged upon as the design for a wide-brimmed hat. (See Fig. 38 B, while Fig. 23 B shows its first arrangement.)

Obviously the most drastic change in men's clothes was that from a somewhat loosely shaped garment into a figure-fitting 'gipon',

B

1330

A

1345

C

1375

Fig. 23

almost skin-tight in its most exaggerated interpretations. These 'gipons' were cut on the scantiest of lines, sometimes barely covering the buttocks in their most modish representations. The hose had naturally become very elongated to correspond with the abbreviation of the 'gipon', but were still separate; it was not until about 1380 that they reached the waist and assumed the proportions of tights.

Several passing fashions occurred in masculine attire during the early years of the fourteenth century. The 'garnache' or loose-fitting tunic with a sort of cape sleeve appeared in the closing years of the thirteenth century and lasted in undiminishing popularity for some

Fig. 24. – 1340

fifty years (Fig. 24). This was usually worn over a fairly long under-tunic, and had a curiously shaped collar-opening finished with two oval flaps.

The fashion for jagged and dagged edges to all garments was essentially a man's prerogative; these edges were cut in a great variety of patterns, from a plain scollop to a very decorative leaf pattern. The entire edge of a cloak or 'gorget', or the loosely hanging sleeves of the 'surcote', which became fashionable about 1325, were nearly always decorated in this manner.

For women too a shift or linen shirt, corresponding to those worn by the men, was the only undergarment. Next came the 'kirtle' or under-gown, tight-fitting to the hips, the back and later the front laced to make it fit closer and the sleeves buttoned from wrist to elbow. The outer gown was referred to alike as a 'cote hardie' or surcoat and was, more often than not, sleeveless.

One of the most typical styles, introduced in the late 40's to last in popularity for over a century, was the cut-away 'cote hardie' (Fig.

Fig. 25. – 1350

25). This garment was the elaborate outcome of the sleeveless gown worn during the previous century. The apertures which had once served as arm-holes were cut away to such an extreme that they showed the belt worn on the hips of the 'kirtle' beneath. The shoulders were narrowed so that only a strap of two or three inches remained to hold the garment in position. Its vicissitudes can be traced through the succeeding pages.

Fig. 26. – 1350

An important innovation of the time was the extreme use of buttons as an ornamentation as well as for utilitarian purposes. In earlier years the brooch and pin had been almost the only means of fastening. From the fourteenth century onwards, buttons became of primary importance.

The lowered waist-line was a general feature of the fourteenth century. Where, previously, the belt or girdle had been worn at the normal waist, it had now descended to the hips and, about the middle of the century, must have been extremely difficult to wear, as it appears to have descended still lower and was composed of weighty metals and precious stones – these were worn by both women and men.

Another style which appeared at this time was the fashion for 'tippets' – bands of material, usually white, some three or four inches wide and worn above the elbow, falling in a long streamer almost to the hem of the gown (Fig. 27). On the same figure the use of 'fichets' will be noticed. These pocket-like slits in garments, worn by both

1330   1380

Fig. 27.

men and women, became a feature of the 'surcote' during the closing years of the thirteenth century, their use being as a means of access to the belt worn on the 'kirtle' or 'gipon', where purse and knife were kept.

Some years before the middle of the fourteenth century the sleeves were extended over the hand, in some cases to the knuckle and cut closely fitting but not rucked at the wrist.

Many were the changes wrought in the matter of women's head-dress throughout this century. During the opening years the wimple or chin veil was extensively worn, both by old and young women; it was a fashion that took many years to become totally obliterated, and we may still see the elderly and restrained wearing it well into the sixteenth century. Fig. 27 A shows three different arrangements of the wimple in its earlier stages.

A very interesting type of head veil became fashionable about 1360; this was one with layers of ruched or goffered frills sewn along the front straight edge of a half-circle of material, the weight

Fig. 28. – 1380

of the frills holding it closely round the face and forming an inverted U (Fig. 29 A), and coming down to the jaw-bone on either side of the face; sometimes the veil was also ornamented with a similar row of frills at the back. This shape became even more popular towards the close of the century; another headdress was evolved from it, giving much the same effect, though not to be confused with its original inspiration, which was only an ornamented veil. Fig. 35 shows the padded cushion-like affair which was held in place by its attachment to the circlet. Usually this was covered with the all-popular gold mesh and jewels, and was called the reticulated coif-fure, as the hair was worn inside it.

Another very popular method of adorning the head was the circlet, with an open-work casing at each side of the face (Fig. 27); the hair was plaited and folded into these cases which were in front

Fig. 29 A. – 1370   Fig. 29 B

of the ears; this fashion was distinctive of the middle of the fourteenth century.

In the year 1383 Anne of Bohemia married Richard II, and introduced into England some of the most extraordinary headdresses in
the history of the world. Before this date practically all headdresses
had been inspired either as a covering for the hair, or as a means of
drawing attention to its beauty; now the one consuming idea was to
cover all traces of the fact that a woman had any hair on her head
at all! This scheme was carried to such an excess that even the hairs
on the neck had to be removed, and it became quite a common sight
to see a lady of quality plucking out the hairs on her neck as she
listened to her minstrels, or watched a tournament.

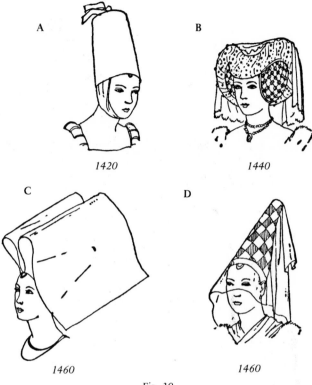

A 1420

B 1440

C 1460

D 1460

Fig. 30

So numerous were the varieties of headdresses introduced in the closing years of the fourteenth century and throughout the fifteenth, that there is not the space to deal with each of these with any degree of thoroughness. There are, however, sufficient drawings in the ensuing pages to illustrate the most popular forms of headgear. It was an age of fantastic decoration, and the woman who devised a new method of adorning her head, be it with horns, pads or boxes, or of course a new variety of hennin or sugar-loaf, was immediately fashionable; apparently the more absurd and inhuman the encumbrance, the more in vogue the wearer became.

Nor indeed were the revolutionary ideas exclusive to headdress. A passion for over-decoration and general exaggeration of already known shapes was accentuated by the introduction of an entirely new silhouette; this was known as the Houpelande. The masculine and feminine interpretation of the same garment can be seen in Figs 33 A and B. This houpelande was a voluminous gown cut from

1446   1470

1420   1420

Fig. 31

Fig. 32. – 1439

a complete circular piece of material with long, pointed, hanging sleeves. The general effect thus being of a gown close at the throat, fitting the top of the shoulders, and thence falling in folds of ever-increasing fullness to the hem. When worn by men the houpelande

A   B

Fig. 33. – 1420

fitted the throat well up to the ears, and was more often than not decorated with a band of fur; it was practically always belted, but no rules governed the length it might be worn, from mid-thigh to the ground. With the use of the houpelande came the high waist for women. A wide belt, four to six inches in width, was worn close

Fig. 34. – 1400

under the breasts; this fashion outlived the popularity of its instigator, the houpelande, and we find it still fashionable well into the sixteenth century. The introduction of a high waist-line, however, did not detract from the general popularity of the sideless gown, nor the closely fitting kirtle from shoulder to hip; these two fashions found their adherents until about 1480, when they were entirely supplanted by the universal high or normal waist-line.

Other features of the closing years of the fourteenth century were

Fig. 35. – 1400

the added emphasis of the width of shoulder, a numerous variety in sleeves, a passion for tall and peculiar hats, and the ridiculous elongation of the toes of shoes; all these styles are easily traceable to their origin in the court of the young Richard II and Anne of Bohemia.

There are several things that stand out with emphasis in the fifteenth century, the chief of which appears to be in the wealth of colour and design. The use of patterns as a means of ornamentation succeeded the popularity of barbaric jewellery.

After about 1420 practically every garment was covered with a large design, sometimes so large that only one repeat would appear on the front or back of the very much abbreviated jacket of a fashionable gentleman.

Fig. 36. – 1395

Excess and exaggeration governed every new style, and hardly a single fashion was started that was not carried to a ridiculous extreme within a few years of its introduction.

Perhaps one of the silliest and unpractical crazes was that for long-toed shoes, which reached the height of absurdity in about 1420 when the toes became so long that they had to be attached to the knees with chains, so that they didn't trip the wearer, or someone else who might be passing ; indeed a law was enforced by the nobility prohibiting the use of shoes with points longer than two feet for all those who did not receive an income of over forty pounds per annum ! Thus assuring one excess to be enjoyed by the wealthy alone.

Between the years 1420–50 every shape and size in hats had been tried, large and small brimmed, with immense towering crowns, globular crowns, cottage-loaf crowns, small rolled brims, brims turned up and brims turned down, and eventually the feathered, high-crowned, and small- or no-brimmed hat which achieved a general popularity for about thirty years (Fig. 38 A). And throughout this time the old hood, with its cockscomb and liripipe (the latter now known by the name of tippet) held a sort of dignified aloofness.

Fig. 37. – 1408

In Fig. 39 this headdress, now often called a bonnet, has the shape, which was originally formed by the liripipe, made into a solid roll; this roll was termed a roundlet.

In the same figure a newer type of jacket is to be seen; this differed

from those worn earlier in the century, in that the neck-line was
cut in a V shape front and back, and showed the high collar of the
doublet underneath, whilst those worn from the end of the fourteenth century to about 1430 had the high collar actually on the
outer gown or jacket as they were now called.

From about 1420 to 1480 the emphasis in shape was on the
shoulders and hips; the shoulders were all enlarged by the addition
of full padded sleeves, or a single roll at the top of the sleeve; in
the former case the sleeve was made very long and fairly loose fitting,
a slit sometimes at the elbow, where the arm could come out if so
desired; if the entire length of sleeve was worn on the arm the
fullness was folded between the elbow and wrist, and was so long as

A   B

Fig. 38. – 1440

Fig. 39. – 1440   Fig. 40. – 1460

barely to show the finger-tips (Fig. 39). Fig. 40 shows the sleeve with the slit top.

The emphasis on the hips was obtained by a very full skirt, and an exceedingly tight belt, and later, by judicious gathering at the front and back as seen on Fig. 41.

Some years before the 80's the idea of points became prevalent. This method of joining a variety of assorted parts of a dress, by making holes and tying them together with ties somewhat resembling a boot-lace, carried right through the time of the Tudors and well into the Stuarts. In this example (Fig. 41 B) the sleeve of the gipon is slit and tied showing the shirt underneath, and the sleeve

B

A

Fig. 41. – 1468

Fig. 42. – 1470

Fig. 43. – 1482

of the doublet is quite separate from the doublet itself, but tied in a corresponding manner by points at the shoulders. During the 80's the slowly receding doublet became so ridiculously abbreviated that it was barely long enough to belt at the waist, and after this date it is quite usual to see the doublet hanging from the shoulders without any belt (Figs 42 and 43).

Chapter 3

EARLY TUDORS, HENRY VII TO ELIZABETH—1485 to 1558

The early Tudor styles were as intriguing as they were fantastic. Henry VII's reign witnessed the somewhat drastic change from extreme brevity to voluminous excess in men's clothes, and the first

Fig. 44. – 1490

appearance of a full-gathered skirt for women, in contrast to the flared and circular ones of the Middle Ages.

Although neither of these styles was definitely established as the general rule until the reign of Henry VIII (1509), we can find a very distinct tendency towards the voluminous even in the transitionary stages.

Throughout the reign of Henry VII women's hair was frequently worn loose, or in a net or snood reminiscent of the crespin of the thirteenth and fourteenth centuries; this style in itself was something in the nature of a revolution, after the hairless and gigantic head-coverings which had been in favour for the preceding 100 years. The hennin or sugar-loaf headdress was still to be seen in diminishing quantities until about 1500, but as will be seen in Fig. 46, even this had changed its whole nature and effect, in its angle and the addition of long lappets hanging down on either side of the face; these had been added some time during the 70's, and were perhaps the original inspiration of a fashion for so framing the face, which is one of the definite characteristics of the early Tudor styles, especially in England.

A   B

Fig. 45. – 1490

A   B

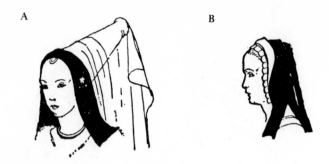

Fig. 46. – 1490

Contemporary portraits of Elizabeth of York show her wearing the Gable or Kennel headdress, a sombre note in head-covering in comparison with the excesses of the preceding century. This head-dress in its original arrangement (Fig. 47) was worn for some fifteen years, and later rearranged, as will be seen in Fig. 49, with the flaps folded neatly back over the gable, and the veil, which was divided at the back, arranged to suit the wearer. This veil, as can be seen in Fig. 46 B, was nearly always split at either side, forming three sections, one at the back and one over either shoulder.

When the Gable headdress was first worn, the hair was just parted in the middle and allowed to fall free at the back, beneath the veil; later, about 1510, when the rearrangement took place, the hair was either bound with ribbons and folded across the forehead, or else covered by cases of striped silk. This, crossed over a striped base, formed an essential part of the general effect and filled the gap from the head to the protruding edge of the jewelled or embroidered coif, which made the structural shape of the headdress. About 1500–5 a close-fitting coif, surmounted by a circlet of jewels (Fig. 48 A) and worn with the same short veil behind, became popular. This style was enlarged upon and exaggerated until it assumed the proportions of a bonnet (Fig. 54) and became so heavy with jewelled decorations that it had to be tied beneath the chin to keep it from slipping off the head.

To follow the German style in clothes and hats of all kinds was distinctly the fashion from about 1500 to 1535, and that is why at this particular period we see two definite styles in the headdresses and clothes of women.

On the one hand, the adherents to the English fashion wore the gables and coifs, with a gown with full trailing skirts, huge bell-

Fig. 47. — 1500

shaped sleeves, square necks, and a solid bolster-like shaping from waist to armpits, which was brought about by the use of leather corsets (Fig. 47).

And on the other hand those who followed the prevailing German styles wore the hair loosely in a net, surmounted by a masculine hat well adorned with feathers, and worn at a jaunty angle. An exceedingly high waist, and a very low-cut neckline, usually oval in shape, leaving the bodice only a few inches in depth, full slashed sleeves, cut and puffed and tied in a bewildering number of ways, and an even fuller and more voluminous skirt gathered to the waist in great thick folds almost resembling pleats in their extreme fullness (Fig. 52 A).

Fig. 48. – 1520

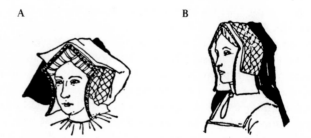

A   B

Fig. 49. – 1515

Fig. 50. – 1530

Men's attire, at this particular period, passes from the simplicity of three garments to the eccentricities of a dozen. So complicated and numerous were the additions of fronts, shirts, sleeves, etc., after about 1500, that in many cases it is impossible to discover just what this or that part had in connexion with the rest of the ensemble.

Fig. 51 A and B show the change of fifteenth- to sixteenth-century silhouettes with the maximum of simplicity. If we take the standard garments as a doublet and jerkin — the doublet worn next to the shirt, the jerkin outside — we have some foundation to work upon. The doublet, as worn during the opening years of the century, was little more than an abbreviated waistcoat, made with or without sleeves; these could be attached to any garment by the already popular method of tying with points (Fig. 51 B and C). Sometimes the jerkin was exactly similar in cut — with the addition of sleeves — or again it might be full-skirted as in Fig. 51 B. Tights, called stocks, were worn by all, and were tied to the doublet.

If the doublet were only short, reaching to the waist, a separate skirt would be added. The shirt was perhaps the only garment that was not cut up into several different pieces, and from about 1485

A

1495

B

1510

C

D

Fig. 51

until 1520 remained practically unchanged. It was very full, the fullness gathered into a low neck-line sometimes almost off the shoulders, and the sleeves profusely gathered at the shoulder and again at the wrist and finished with a small frill. After 1520 the neck-line was drawn up round the throat and again finished with a frill – the germ of the ruffle to come. This fashion, however, was not generalized until about 1540, the low neck-line still finding favour.

A   B

Fig. 52. – 1530

Worn over the doublet and jerkin was an exceedingly full, knee-length gown; this gown varied little in shape from about 1500 until about 1560. It was quite often lined with fur or velvet, or some such contrasting material. A deep fur collar, turned back at the neck, added to the height and width of already over-accentuated shoulders. Usually the gown had short sleeves, or a long sleeve cut open on the outside, and left hanging (Fig. 55 B). But quite often it had no

Fig. 53. — 1495

sleeves at all. The back of the gown was gathered on to a yoke; this
may be seen in Fig. 53, but the yoke was considerably higher than
this example in the ensuing years.

The 30's and 40's saw these gowns — and indeed the jerkin and
other masculine garments — made with so much fullness that not
another fold could be pushed into the seams, and in many cases the
bulk was so great that the folds were just caught in loops on to the
seam and actually stood away from the garment in a series of corru-
gated pleats. This excessive fullness, however, was more a characteristic of the German garments than those worn in England.

Every garment was slashed and bombasted and generally over-
ornamented, the chief means of adornment being bands of velvet
called 'guards', and the profuse addition of jewels and embroideries
to the already almost priceless materials. Henry VIII's reign was

distinguished for its excesses, and the richness of the gowns is hardly believable unless studied in the contemporary portraits of the period. Silks and velvets, cloth of gold and silver, and brilliantly dyed fabrics lost much of their splendour with the profusion of exotic ornamentation that adorned them. The whole idea of slashing was obviously started so that he who possessed a fine silk shirt and a gorgeous doublet might show his neighbours the magnificence of his undergarments – with dignity.

At what exact date the first farthingale made its début in England is difficult to discover. We can see it first in Spain pictured by artists some time in the 1460's where it was obviously a court extravagance. It is probable that Katharine of Aragon brought the fashion with her from Spain at the beginning of the century but reserved it entirely for state occasions. It was not seen in use in England until

Fig. 54. – 1540

some time in the 40's or 50's. Known as the Spanish Farthingale this hooped skirt was eminently suitable to display the rich damasks and finely worked embroideries so typical of the middle of the century. The gown itself was now tightly fitted over a corset of leather or steel reaching from shoulder to waist with a slight point in front. The skirts were flared and gathered at the waist-line and left open in the front to display an inverted V of some other fabric of rich design. Sleeves were various but during the 30's and 40's they followed a curious tendency which included two separate cuffs, if they can be termed so. The sleeve from shoulder to about half-way down the upper arm was tight fitting and made from the same material as the gown itself. From this short sleeve depended another, bell shaped and made from some contrasting and stiffened fabric falling open half way down the forearm to reveal yet another under-sleeve which could be decorated in various ways, was sometimes slashed to show the sleeve of the shift through each opening and had a tiny frill at the wrist. This particular cuff was shaped tight at the wrist and wide at the elbow (Fig. 54).

Generally the bodice remained cut square at the neck-line to show off an elegant shift or to be covered by a velvet yoke collar or small shoulder cape (Fig. 50).

This particular tightness from waist to under the arms was due no doubt to the stays and is characteristic of the middle years of the century, and a peculiar solidity appears in all contemporary paintings, giving an air of unnaturalness to the ladies.

The high-necked shirt became universal with both men and women after 1550; the top edge was worn in a miniature ruffle and called a partlet strip. As will be seen in Fig. 55 A, the shape of the sleeve had entirely changed from the loose bell form, with the stiffened under-sleeve (Fig. 54), to a tight-fitting one with large padded puffs at the shoulder. This latter shape remained fashionable well into the 80's. The square neck-line introduced at the end of the fifteenth century remained in favour until the closing years of Elizabeth's reign.

It will be noticed that although the flat cap, square-toed shoes, wide shoulders and huge padded sleeves formed the universal outline to the masculine silhouette from 1500 to 1550, slight changes were taking place in the smaller details, such as the slowly descending waist-line and the ascending height of the neck-line, also the gradual appearance of the trunk-hose.

The trunk-hose were, in their first interpretation, formed by the slashing of the upper part of the long hose; later the same effect with added magnificence was obtained by the addition of strips of embroidery. It is an essential feature of the sixteenth century that these garments were normally worn all in one piece; the upper part or breeches was called the upper-stocks, and the lower part, that covering the foot, calf and thigh, called nether-stocks. The ribbons formed by the slashing were called 'panes'. In their earliest forms the spaces between the panes were stuffed with a silk or satin lining, which could be drawn out through the slits, but later as the century advanced these gave place to ridiculous paddings of horsehair and rags covered by some gorgeous material, until the effect was one of a gigantic roll round the hips.

The full-skirted waistcoat or doublet − or the added full skirt − gave place to the straight doublet seen in Fig. 55 B about 1550, and

A B

Fig. 55. − 1556

Fig. 56. – 1555

a few years later started to lose its skirts entirely (Fig. 56). This example shows the upper-stocks with a tight-fitting hip-yoke typical of these garments in their early stages of advancement. The panes cut slantwise and embroidered and reaching only from the top of the leg – later we see them cut to the waist – the new doublet or jerkin without skirts, and the 'mock-coat', a cloak with imitation sleeves, are all fashions directly traceable to the Spanish influence during Queen Mary's reign. The influence of Philip of Spain on the English traditional costume was marked to a degree. Although many men still adhered to the old German styles with their wide padded shoulders and knee-length gowns, the new idea of a fitting doublet and a short cape or mock-coat was definitely establishing itself with a precedence.

From 1553 until the accession of Elizabeth in 1558, women's clothes changed hardly at all. Mary clung tenaciously to the fashion of her father's court, and except for the bodice, or stomacher as it was called, being cut to a V shape instead of the straight line in front,

and the already-mentioned change in sleeves, little or nothing happened to change the silhouette. With headdresses, however, there
certainly were several changes during the early 50's. The circular
coif or caul headdress, already described (Fig. 54), lost popularity
due to its extreme weight and discomfort, and little close-fitting
caps, beautifully embroidered, were for some years the foundation
of most designs in headdresses. Over these were worn the masculine
cap or hat, and also the heart-shaped cap associated with that
unhappy Queen, Mary Queen of Scots.

Before the close of this chapter it is necessary perhaps to say one
or two things in regard to footwear. During the closing years of the
fifteenth century the hose with felt or leather soles – worn during
the latter Middle Ages – gave place to a round-toed slipper, like a
mule, with no heel. This, later, for reasons of practicability, was
tied with strings round the ankle, and about 1510 had about one
inch covering at the heel. The toe then became square and padded,
following the traditional tendencies of the period, linings being
drawn out through slashings across the toes. Soft coloured leather
boots were worn for riding from the beginning of the period until
about 1540. The fashion for square toes somewhat abated during
the 50's and an altogether higher-cut shoe took its place, slightly
pointed or rounded at the toe and with a turned-back 'collar' at the
ankle. Slashings were still the vogue.

Chapter 4

ELIZABETH TO JAMES I
1558 to 1625

The opening years of Queen Elizabeth's reign witnessed the decline and fall of the old order of headdresses, finished at the back with a veil. And also saw the general adoption of a cap or bonnet as a head-covering which was to stay in favour, with few interruptions, until the beginning of the nineteenth century.

Fig. 57 A, B and C show the new though transitory styles adopted during the 60's and early 70's; a certain flatness was the general

Fig. 57. – 1555–70

tendency in direct contrast to the circular cauls of a few years earlier. The heart-shaped bonnet eventually became the most popular form of headdress, and with this the old style of hairdressing departed. No longer was the hair parted in the middle, and worn smoothly drawn across the brow, but it was brushed back from the forehead, puffed at the sides, waved and padded to fill the gaps formed by the double curve. (See Fig. 57 A and D.)

And later still, from about 1585, the hair was fuzzed, crimped and curled over wire frames. Indeed, from 1580 to the death of Anne of Denmark, 1619, the hair received more attention than it had since the twelfth century. Dyeing was generally fashionable, red or saffron being the favourite shades, pads and switches of false hair were arranged over the wire frames to add to an insufficient natural supply, and wigs became increasingly fashionable. Elizabeth herself was supposed to have owned several hundred at this time. No attempt at naturalness was aimed at, and certainly none achieved; a fashionable lady might appear at successive functions with a different-coloured head of hair for each occasion if she could afford such a luxury. Wreaths and borders and tiny caps were worn, and the hair became the nesting-place for countless rings, jewels and pearls that could not be judiciously affixed elsewhere about the person.

Large beaver and velvet caps, richly ornamented and trimmed with feathers, were perched at a precarious and jaunty angle on top of the complicated hairdressing.

For those of more modest inclination little embroidered caps or bonnets were normally worn over the hair both to keep it back from the face and to furnish a stabilizer for the hats when worn. There are many charming examples of such bonnets or coifs in the Victoria and Albert Museum.

Numerous, indeed, were the changes that took place during the 60's, and the introduction of new ideas found favour in the eyes of a young queen. One of the most charming styles adopted at this period was that for a flared, puff-sleeved mantle, which was worn over the kirtle and gown (Fig. 58), and hung straight from the shoulders in deep folds, increasing in fullness towards the hem. This mantle was trimmed with wide bands of velvet or embroideries, pearls or jewels being added on those worn by the wealthy. The short full sleeve was finished at the elbow with a tight band.

And yet another step in the advancement of fashionable details was the introduction of starch in 1564. As every young woman of fashion took lessons in the art of starching, the style for ruffles be-

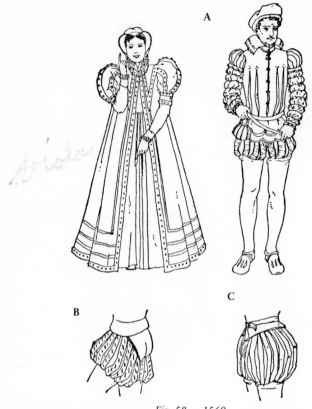

Fig. 58. – 1560

came widespread. The great problem of stiffening them having been successfully negotiated, there was no obvious check to the increase in size and competition in this direction, and from about 1570 until 1620 ruffles and collars grew to startling proportions.

The earliest form of starch used in this country was yellow in tone, imparting a somewhat rich creamy shade to the material. This colour was only fashionable, however, for a few years, and after the hanging of a notorious woman wearing a 'yellow ruff', the starch changed its tone to blue, which tint it has retained to this day.

The square-cut gown typical of the early Tudors did not entirely lose favour throughout the century but after the 60's it was not universal, and frequently the bodice or stomacher came right up to the throat. Neither did the introduction of the puffed shoulder and tight sleeve deter from the general popularity of the full, bombasted and slashed sleeves. These, indeed, attained even greater dimensions during the 90's than at any previous date, and, if possible, even more luxuriant ornamentation.

During the late 70's an entirely new contour was introduced with the French farthingale. This farthingale consisted·of a hoop, several feet in diameter, fixed to the waist with a series of tapes, the whole tilted down in the front (Figs 60 A and 62 B). The skirt worn over this was of necessity exceedingly full, the gathers radiating from the waist of the stomacher like the sun's rays. Sometimes a sort of basque was worn over the skirt reaching to the edge of the hoop, and later during the 90's a gigantic ruffle, in magnified repitition to the one at the throat, was worn resting upon the hoop.

As in the case of most extreme fashions, some less exaggerated form had to be introduced to fill the requisites of the more modest minded, and a sort of semicircular bolster was introduced for this purpose, which tied with tapes in front, over the petticoat but under the gown itself; these skirts were always split up the front, showing a contrasting underskirt in movement.

A   B

Fig. 59. – 1575

Fig. 60. – 1585

With the new French silhouette the stomacher became elongated to a point about eight or ten inches below the waist in front. A more restricting corset was introduced to give the added flatness below the waist. This V-shaped stomacher was stiffened and often worn at a slight angle to the body, fitting closely at the breast but sloping away from the waist and resting its point on the tilted front of the farthingale. In some cases it must have been an entirely false front to the gown, as there are contemporary portraits which show the hands hidden behind it. The 80's and 90's showed the fashion in its extreme, when the human figure appears distorted beyond recognition and tight-lacing was accentuated by the addition of bolsters above and below the corset.

The insistence of brilliant gewgaws, pearls and precious stones of

Fig. 61. – 1587

all kinds predominates throughout the century, but the last twenty years show a lack of design in their profuse use. Odd brooches and pins and hair adornments seem to have been attached at random. Quantities of rings and necklaces and ear-rings proclaimed the wealth of their wearers, but no comprehensive attempt at simplicity as a background for wealth seems to have been attempted. Those who followed the French styles let themselves go wholeheartedly into an elaborate orgy of luxuriance and dazzling decoration.

Here again we find the two entirely different outlines that were fashionable at the same time; the Spanish influence still held sway and, as will be seen in Fig. 61, presented a marked contrast to Fig. 60, which is comparatively the same date. The short slightly pointed stomacher, plain sleeves with the emphasis at the shoulder, and the bell-shaped skirt vied in popularity with the more exotic styles just described.

Spanish

French

1599

Fig. 62 A

Fig. 62 B

Fig. 63 A. – 1587   *Fig. 63 B. – 1570*

Men's fashions started to change with startling rapidity during the 60's; between 1560 and 1620 practically every conceivable shape in breeches had made its appearance.

As the doublet became shorter more attention was paid to the trunk-hose. It will be clearly seen in Fig. 58 B and C that the panes started from the hips at the side and generally reached to mid-thigh, they were stuffed with an assortment of rags and horse-hair and exaggerated to the nth degree, until they resembled a giant pumpkin in contour. The assortment of rubbish that went to their stuffing was discreetly covered with a lining of some fine material, which could be drawn out at will through the panes, forming a contrast in its puckered gatherings (Fig. 64 B).

A

B

Fig. 64. – 1595

Venetians, a sort of padded and quilted knee-breeches (Figs 63 B and 65) came into fashion in this country about 1572. They were worn with a short nether-stock and usually tied at the knee with a wide ribbon.

Continental fashions were being introduced into England in a bewildering variety, and at such a speed that the would-be gallant had an impossible standard of finery to contend with and was perpetually out of fashion. However, some satisfaction must have been gained in the fact that although one new fashion temporarily eclipsed that of a previous year's, when it was established the styles of an earlier date once more made their appearance.

Fig. 60 B shows yet another type of leg-covering; these were called trunk-hose with canions, the canion being the tight-fitting extension covering the thigh. Separate nether-stocks were worn over these. A further arrangement of the same idea can be seen in Fig. 64. This squareness must have been obtained with the help of wires. A and B show the distinctive contours – one with the panes worn neatly arranged outside, the other with the lining pulled through in puffs completely concealing the panes. This square-shaped trunk-hose was not worn until the 90's.

Fig. 63 A shows the 'open breechers', which made their appearance during the 80's but did not become particularly fashionable. The same idea was introduced again some fifty years later and met with approval and general adoption in the nether-garments of the cavalier.

Breeches as leg coverings, worn from the waist down, could be almost any length from about 1570 onwards. That the peasants tended to wear slops or long loose trousers rather than the fancy breeches of the wealthy is understandable for it must have taken the ingenuity of a genius to construct some of the shapes with their bombasted linings and interlinings, their puffs and paddings at hip or thigh.

Having dealt at some length upon the eccentricities of the nether-garments of Elizabethan England, we will now return to the doublets and coats.

With the advancement of the 70's the doublet began to swell, with startling rapidity, into a point over the stomach. This very hideous fashion assumed the proportion of a gigantic hooked nose, the tip of the 'nose' projecting several inches beyond and below the belt. It was very aptly termed the peascodbelly doublet (Figs 59 B and 60 B). This fashion reached its most exaggerated and ridiculous

Fig. 65. – 1595

form during the late 80's, and after that date slowly shrank back to normal, and at the close of Elizabeth's reign, 1602, had entirely disappeared.

After this fashion had somewhat abated in its deformity, the 'skirts' of the doublet once more made their appearance, and were cut up into square flaps called 'tassets' – the easier to fit over the gigantic trunk-hose and breeches of the time (Figs 66 and 69).

If the sleeves were not shaped in the full padded style, they were usually finished at the shoulder with 'wings' or rolls of material or 'picadils'.

These 'picadils' should have been explained earlier in the book, at the time of their introduction about 1520. They were a form of

Fig. 66. – 1612

ornamentation which lasted with unchallenged popularity till the close of the Tudor dynasty; and consisted of a tubular roll of material cut at equal intervals almost severing the tube, and worn only on curved surfaces so that the slits might be pulled apart, leaving each separate section of tube standing up in a minute roll. This can be seen under the ruffle in Fig. 58 and on the shoulders of Figs 61 and 66. Hanging sleeves from the shoulders formed the fashion from 1580 till the late 30's of the seventeenth century, and were worn by both sexes (Figs 61, 62 and 67).

Short cloaks and mock-coats were worn universally throughout this period, and a long loose gown with hanging sleeves, heavily decorated with braid and embroideries, was worn as a sort of informal dress – and by elderly gentlemen – from about 1575 to

Fig. 67. – 1616

Fig. 68. – 1610

1620 (Fig. 68). These gowns were often lined with fur or shag, a rough woollen material.

At about the same time that women's hairdressing became complicated and exaggerated, men started to wear theirs long again. First to the lobe of the ear, then shoulder-length, and about 1595 a fashion for 'ear-locks', later called love-locks, became very popular for the younger generation. These locks were worn only in front, the back hair remaining short. Probably because the high collars and ruffles interfered too much with hair longer than a short 'bob'.

Hats of various shapes and sizes were worn during the whole of this period, 1558 to 1623. They were made from a variety of imported materials, including felt, beaver and velvet of practically every hue – and as long as they were trimmed with a band or cord, lace or jewels, any shape might be worn.

Fig. 69. – 1615

Fig. 70. – 1611

In 1556 Queen Mary made a half-hearted attempt to revive the collapsing wool trade in England by ordering every man with an income of less than £40 to wear a woollen cap. This decree had no noticeable effect on the fashions in headgear and the hat continued in popularity, reaching its highest crown about 1595 (Fig. 65).

Ornament was the particular excess of all Tudor costume but during the early years of the century such ornament took the form of richly decorated imported fabrics – damasks, silks and velvets with ornate designs of foreign origin and brilliant contrasts as well as slashings and 'drawings out', furs and feathers, bands and guards and most popular of all gold lace on a black velvet ground.

Fig. 71. – 1610

During Elizabeth I's reign the concentration on exaggerated shapes, which was a desire to provide an even greater surface for decoration, produced the farthingale, bombasted sleeves and breeches. Each garment could be stiffened to present a more interesting surface for embroideries or other forms of ornament. Gigantic ruffles and collars propped up at the back of the neck to make a higher frame for the face were decorated with gold lace, coloured pins and occasionally the odd jewel that could not be accommodated anywhere else on the body of the gown.

Eventually, towards the end of the century, fantastic hoods to frame the whole body made their appearance. Sometimes these were of transparent lawn with fine lacy edges that not only framed the head in a heart-shaped cover but trailed in deep folds to the ground behind (Fig. 70). Even shoes and hose received the same sort of treatment for both men and women; clocks decorated the legs of the well-dressed man as high as the knee and his shoes were almost obliterated by the gigantic gold lace rosettes which were sewn to the toe of the shoes. In order to show off this new elegance the ladies' dresses became shorter. During James I's reign they were often well above the ankle but there was little change from the already-mentioned styles.

Anne of Denmark favoured the French farthingale in spite of James's repeated onslaught upon its undesirable qualities and not until 1618 does it disappear. Slight modifications in the shape of the stomacher took place during the opening years of the seventeenth century. The false V front gave place to a very corseted short V, the neck became very *décolletée*, the breasts frequently visible above the square or rounded corsage, and a deep laced ruff took the place of the smaller one of earlier years. When the ruff was not worn, huge curving collars took its place (Fig. 71 A, B and C).

Chapter 5

CHARLES I TO JAMES II
1625 to 1684

When Charles I came to the throne in 1625, the old styles of Eliza-beth and James I quickly disappeared, giving place to an entirely new outline, the differences being most marked by a new freedom and negligence, which governed practically all the styles at this time. The bombast and general stiffness which was so typical of these last two reigns was succeeded by a wealth of soft materials – laces, spot muslins, ribbons, dainty patterns – and perhaps most noticeable of all, a studied nonchalance in hairdressing. Soft colourings, pinks and pale blues, succeeded the rather harsh brilliance of a decade ago; embroideries of exquisite fineness adorned the backs of gloves, shoes, sword belts, boot-hose, stockings and the tassets on the doublets (Fig. 75). And in some strange way, the cut of the clothes empha-sized these refinements instead of obliterating them as had previously been the case. This new softness proved the ideal background for exquisite workmanship.

In Fig. 72 A there still remains an armorial air about the cut of the doublet; a padded solidity about the chest, which had quite dis-appeared by 1630. Here in these two figures can be seen the new style in hairdressing which had made its appearance some twenty-five years earlier, but now became more popular and more and more nonchalant in its effect, the back hair rarely reached beyond the top of the collar; but the love-locks were made much of, being tied with bows of ribbon and curled and fizzed to excess. In the more exaggera-ted French styles of the period the hair rather resembled a bird's nest than a head of human hair. Long hair for men had become an established fashion by 1620 to last, in effect, including wigs, of course, for nearly 200 years.

Beards and moustaches were practically always worn, the former being cut in a point, the latter curled and waxed.

With the exception of a leather jerkin (Figs 73 and 76 A), which reached to mid-thigh and was generally worn for some ten or fifteen years, the doublets were all cut to the waist and finished by the addition of the all-popular 'tassets' (Fig. 72 A and B). Later the idea was imitated, as seems to have been the case with an incredible amount of fashions, and the same effect was achieved or attempted with false bows of ribbon, serving no purpose, and mock-tassets (Figs 74 A and 75).

The full short breeches (Figs 74 C and B and 72 A), relics of an earlier period, were still worn in England until about 1627. But the newer French modes embraced slightly full knee-breeches worn just below the knee, the sides buttoned or tied, and during the 20's and early 30's, left undone some four inches above the knee to show the linings at the side (Fig. 72 B and ᴰ). The knees became one of the centres of adornment, and if they were not tied with a wide and

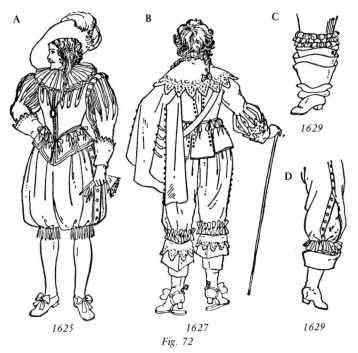

A   B   C

1629

D

1625   1627   1629

Fig. 72

Fig. 73. – 1624

ornate garter, the breeches always finished with bows of ribbon, tassels, lace or ornamentation of some kind. Boots, boot-hose, and decorated stocking-tops played an important rôle in the dress of a gallant from the late 20's till the close of the 60's.

The stocking-tops were worn over the ordinary hose; the habit of wearing two or even three pairs was prevalent from 1625 to the end of the century. Boot-hose had originally served the useful purpose of preventing too much friction from the ill-fitting boots of the period upon the somewhat fragile and extremely expensive hose; now their practicability was challenged by their merits as an entirely decorative furbelow (Fig. 72 B).

The ridiculous bucket-top boot became a necessary part of out-door dress. These were so numerous and variegated in cut and design

Fig. 74. – 1630

that it is quite impossible to give a comprehensive description of all their forms and vagaries. Fig. 72 C shows one of the more exaggerated styles. Nearly always the instep was decorated with an enormous butterfly flap of leather. These boots were the recipients of the satirists' jibes, and were ridiculed and exaggerated by contemporary writers and artists alike – not, however, to their ultimate detriment in the eyes of fashion, for they lasted well in favour until after the Restoration. Sleeves were somewhat varied in design during Charles I's reign – possibly the full sleeve, split up the outside from wrist to shoulder and showing the silk or satin shirt, was the most generally worn, but slashed sleeves, and those composed entirely of loosely hanging ribbons, were almost equally popular.

The most striking and universal items, however, from 1625–50 were the huge lace collars and cuffs immortalized by Van Dyck

Fig. 75. – 1631

These were worn by everyone from king to kitchen-maid. The high-crowned and small-brimmed hats of a preceding quarter of a century vanished amidst an overwhelming popularity for large-brimmed flopping hats decorated lavishly with feathers—another fashion that outlasted the century.

A startling difference will be seen in the women's clothes worn during the first twenty years of the century and those worn after Henrietta Maria came to England, bringing with her the latest thing in French fashions. This complete and rapid change may be accounted for in some sense by the fact that England had no Queen for some seven years, and the Court had entertained no women during that period. With the re-establishment of a Queen—albeit unpopular but nevertheless a Queen – the ladies were quick to mimic the French fashions, and in no period in the history of costume has the change been so completely revolutionary. Gone were the V-shaped stomachers, the bombasted sleeves, the hooped skirts, the curled wigs, the chalked faces and dyed hair, ruffles and thick-soled shoes – all rendered ridiculous by the newer styles in violent contrast.

The stomacher was U-shaped, while it lasted, for some ten years,

A   B

Fig. 76. – 1635

and frequently finished after the masculine style with 'tassets'; the waist-line was very high, several inches above the natural waist in many instances; the skirts were full and soft, still usually split up the front to show the petticoat beneath. The sleeves were rather complex for some five or ten years, the general idea being that the gown had a short split sleeve from elbow to shoulder, and under this a false

Fig. 77. – 1635

sleeve composed entirely of ribbons held in place by the gown sleeve tying just above the elbow, and through the apertures between the ribbons the full sleeves of the 'smock' or undergarment made their appearance (Fig. 77). During the 30's this fashion disappeared, to be supplanted by the full three-quarter-length sleeve (Figs 74 D and 76 B) with huge ruffled cuffs. The first time in the history of English fashion that a woman's forearm was left bare.

Curiously similar styles prevailed in the arrangement of men's and women's hair; except that in the woman's case her hair was done up at the back whilst the man's was cut short. The usual method of doing up the hair was with a circular plait rolled round the back of the head (Fig. 77 A), the curls in the front becoming more and more profuse as the century advanced towards the 70's.

Very essential were such little things as furs and muffs, masks, hoods and veils at this time, and indeed throughout the century; umbrellas also were known after about 1630. John Evelyn bought one in France in 1644.

The high waist was typical only of the 20's and 30's. After 1640 it started once more to assume normal proportions and again tight-lacing became fashionable, and, as seems to have usually been the case with the renewed use of these artifices, the waist began to descend once more to a deep V in front.

The attractive fashion of 'tucked' petticoats, giving a pannier effect, was started towards the close of the 20's, to last without interruption for nearly 100 years. Probably the fashion started with the introduction of a longer skirt, and the shocking condition of the streets brought about by complete lack of drainage necessitated lifting the skirts, which could be more easily managed if pinned or folded up – also in this manner the petticoat beneath could be shown off to fuller advantage.

The 40's, which should in the interests of history be typified by a certain sobriety and decorum in matters of dress, rather shatter one's illusion when studiously examined. If anything the existing contemporary works show an excess of ornament and exaggerated ostentatiousness, accompanied by a brevity of line that is quite inadequate as a background for so much decoration.

Fig. 79 A shows the new cut of coat in one of its more sober moods. Some of these were so brief as to expose several inches of flowing silk shirt between the coat and breeches. They were called 'jackanapes' coats, and the loosely hanging short breeches soon became the full-skirted garments alluded to in Pepys's immortal diary – 'This morning I rose and put on my suit with great skirts . . . Jan. 1, 1659' (Fig. 79 B). The same figure would answer equally well to his description '. . . Black cloth suit trimmed with scarlet ribbon, very neat, and my cloake lined with velvet . . . a new beaver hat which alltogeather is very noble with my black silk knit canions.' Lace was used upon these suits in a bewildering quantity, many of them indeed being laced all over. The sleeves were of almost any length and

A   B

Fig. 78. – 1644

A   1645   B   1660   C   1660

Fig. 79

cut. Possibly those cut at the elbow and finished with a large cuff or bunch of ribbons, so that they showed the masses of silk and lace that did service as a shirt sleeve, were the more popular, though the split sleeve from shoulder to wrist can still be seen in great quantities until the close of the 60's. The bewildering addition of lace and ribbon at the waist, hems, shoulders and toes defies adequate description (Fig. 80). Even the contemporary writers of the time seem somewhat staggered by the extravagances. John Evelyn writes in 1661, 'Clad in the fantastic habits of the time. . . .'

During the late 50's the periwig became fashionable for men. Their natural hair having been curled and crimped and adorned with ribbons to the extent when nature was no longer sufficiently generous for their requirements, the curled periwig with its profusion of ringlets solved the problem. Curious though it may seem, Pepys had his hair cut off in 1663 and made into a periwig, which certainly seems carrying a fashion to unnecessary lengths.

One of the most noticeable changes during the 50's was the

Fig. 80. – 1663

abandonment of the Van Dyck collar in favour of a square stiffened one for men, and later, about 1670, this disappeared, to be replaced by a long lace scarf, worn wound round the neck and tied with a profusion of ribbons under the chin (Fig. 81). The latter style, how-ever, did not occur until some years after the introduction of the

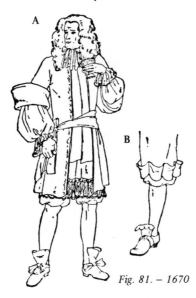

Fig. 81. – 1670

new long coat in 1665. The fashion for the short 'jackanapes' coat had completely gone out by 1668, and the long-skirted one, once firmly established, remained in unchallenged favour for over a century. In its original stages the skirts of the coat were hardly shaped at all, and it hung loosely from the shoulder to display the new garment, the vest or waistcoat; the latter was cut on the same lines, usually with sleeves. The waist was emphasized not by any shaping, but by tying a silk or lace sash over the coat. The breeches changed in style to suit the coat, and instead of being open at the bottom they were gathered in like plus-fours (Fig. 80) and by about 1670 had almost disappeared beneath the skirt of the coat. The tendency to ornament them still remained, however, for a few years. (Fig. 81 A and B).

With the exception of the lowered waist and a rounded neck-line (Fig. 78), and possibly a little more lace and ribbons, the ladies' fashions changed hardly at all until the time of the Restoration. Then for a short period of some ten years, we find the rather peculiar styles of Fig. 82 – a long exaggerated corsage emphasized by the depth of collar, which usually fitted tightly over the shoulders to the elbows, all the fullness of the sleeves had to come beneath this. Should the woman not wish to have her collar to her throat, the one exception seems to have been the extreme reverse, right off the shoulder; but still it must fit snugly over the upper part of the arm

Fig. 82. – 1660

(Fig. 83). False hair was often added at this time to compete to some extent with the ridiculously enlarged heads of the men, and bows of ribbon were usually worn. The 70's marked a new era in ladies' fashions, possibly with the arrival of Charles II's younger sister and Louise de Kéroualle who came to England in 1670 to entice Charles II into coalition with Louis XIV. This famous lady wore her hair in an entirely new style – a style now associated with portraits of Nell Gwynne and paintings by Peter Lely. The sides of the hair were cut and curled and puffed in a mass of ringlets brushed away from the centre parting; the back hair was worn long and arranged over the shoulders in inviting ringlets (Fig. 84). Those who did not care to follow this fashion wore theirs cut fairly short and curled all over, a fringe or 'Fontange' in front and the back tied in a 'boss' or mass of curls at the nape of the neck. Over this was worn a tight-fitting cap with bunches of ribbon in the front, the skeleton of the 'pinner' to come (Fig. 85 A). As these curls took some time to arrange correctly – and inclement weather works havoc on the iron-

Fig. 83. – 1665

Fig. 84. – 1670

wave – scarves and hoods and lace bonnets were used to cover the head when outdoors (Figs 85 B and 86). Not only did the French fashions pertain to hairdressing. Skirts were less full but nearly always ornamented at the hem, and the outer gown assumed the dignity of a train. In many cases this 'train' was entirely separate, being fastened on to the petticoat-bodice across the back; it was always worn folded up, except for special occasions (Fig. 85 A). The tight-lacing was less stiff and more curved, the convex shaping pushing the breasts upwards and leaving a ridge at the top of the corsage, to be discreetly covered with a rather informal arrangement of lace fichu – in direct contrast to the ∩ -shaped shoulders

A   B

C

Fig. 85. – 1670

Fig. 86. – 1680

of the previous decade. The sleeves of the gown were always short, showing the excessive fullness of the silk and laced smock beneath.

Tiny floral patterns decorated nearly all the materials; sometimes these were painted on to the 'taffetys' and 'tabbys' but more often embroidered with painstaking realism. Ribbons and lace were used in a bewildering profusion on all the items in a lady's wardrobe.

One other fashion worthy of note was the general use of paint and powder, patches and lip-rouge, introduced during the 50's, possibly in blatant defiance of the bigoted Protector. John Evelyn remarks its general adoption in 1654.

Chapter 6

JAMES II TO GEORGE III
1685 to 1760

This chapter is split into two distinct sections, from 1685 to 1714 and 1714–60.

The clothes women wore during the last three Stuart reigns were as distinct from those worn at the Courts of the German Georges as any two consecutive fashions could be.

The sudden change can best be remarked by the study of the works of the late Peter Lely and Godfrey Kneller, in contrast to those of Hogarth and Watteau. Curiously enough, all the artists of the late Stuart period favoured a pseudo-classic style of dress, rather than the somewhat formal fashion so typical of the day. For this reason the contemporary portraiture is sadly lacking in authentic representation of the everyday garments that were then in use.

By about 1685 the low curved waist-line had disappeared in preference to a normal one; the petticoat-bodice was made tightly fitting the figure, and usually laced down the front with ribbons, in contrast to the loose sleeve with big 'cuffs' at the elbow. Skirts were fuller again and the bunched-up petticoat was still fashionable to the end of the century. Tiny patterns, spots, plaids and stripes were all exceedingly fashionable (Figs 87 and 88 B).

Long gloves of kid and chamois were nearly always worn out-doors, covering the forearm made bare by the increasingly short sleeves.

About 1690 the folded and bunched train at the back of the gown suggested a new silhouette, and the first bustle made its appearance. This was not composed of wires as was the case in the better-known

Fig. 87. – 1688

bustle of 1870, but a very similar effect was obtained by a padded roll tied across the waist at the back under the petticoat. A curious kind of waistcoat or corset also made its appearance during the 90's (Fig. 89 A). This was braced and stiffened with embroideries, and resembled armour of a grotesque and richly decorated style. Quite often it was worn outside the entire gown, but more often over the chemisette or smock, as a sort of morning deshabille.

Curiously enough this armorial air penetrated into all forms of decoration during the 90's. The decoration of garments, instead of being ribbons and lace, favoured ornate designs resembling iron-work, gold and silver thread and thick gold fringes and tassels being intermittently enlivened by the addition of jewels and semi-precious stones. Buckles and large paste brooches, lockets and hair ornaments came back into fashion after an interval of about eighty years.

1685   1687

Fig. 88

It was also about 1685 that the informality in women's hair-dressing was supplanted by an eccentric fashion which lasted some fifteen or twenty years, practically to the exclusion of any other styles. This was a cap or bonnet, with various etceteras – generally termed the 'commode'. Of the several items that went to the com-position of this headdress, the 'pinner' or 'settee' played the most important part, this being a starched and pleated frill arranged on wires to stand up in front – to be seen clearly in Fig. 89 B, C, D and E.

Fig. 89 B shows the 'settee' or double pinner. A bunch of ribbon was tied behind the pinner (Figs 89 B, C and E) and called a sorti; sometimes another was added in front.

So complex were the varieties and arrangements of the 'commode', and as every item of the whole had its French title, it is impossible to devote the space requisite to its entire explanation in so brief a volume. It is quite definite, however, that this headdress could be worn in parts or in its fullest arrangement with equal correctitude for formal or informal occasions. Thus a 'Flandan' or 'Frelange' – meaning the pinner joined to the bonnet – might be worn at the same social gathering as the pinner and sorti (Fig. 89 E) alone.

Fig. 89. – 1690

During the 80's the hair arrangement beneath the commode did not receive the attention that it did during the 90's; it was sufficient for it to be drawn back from the face with a few curls visible, the back hair often done up (Fig. 89 E). But about '89 a sort of standardized arrangement took place, and every would-be fashionable lady had to study carefully the trend of fashion which demanded a uniformity which was truly absurd (Fig. 89 A, B and D).

Each curl had its allotted position and title; thus the two 'horns' curled up in front from the forehead were called 'Frontange' after Madame Frontange, Louis XIV's mistress, and were supported by a wire called a 'palisade'. (These horns are typical features of the head-dress of the 90's, and the first ten years of the following century, for both men and women.)

Next the 'Passague' or curled locks either side of the temples; 'Confidets', the curls in front of the ears; the 'Chevre Cœur' or heart-breakers, being the curls at the nape of the neck; and lastly, should any small curls escape on the forehead, they were called 'cruches'. The whole arrangement could be finished with the addition of pearls and enamel ornaments set between the horns. One cannot believe that this was one of the fashions which added to a woman's attrac-tions, and the further addition of 'mouches' or patches in lavish quantities and numerous designs could hardly have enhanced her beauty. However, the fashion lasted for several years, and even after the abandonment of the pinner in its towering dignity (about 1705), the same mode of hairdressing remained until the death of Queen Anne.

Men's fashions from this time onwards (1685) ceased to change with the startling rapidity typical of the earlier years of the century, and apart from slight alterations, such as a longer sleeve, fuller skirts, bigger cuffs, and a rearrangement from time to time of the neck-tie or cravat, remained fundamentally the same for some sixty years.

The enlargement of the periwig was one of the most noticeable tendencies of the late 80's. This followed the styles adopted by women in its curled uniformity (Figs 90 B and C and 92). But as will be noticed in Fig. 90 C, the back was usually separated into two thick masses of curls at the bottom and a flatness extending over the back of the head to meet the mass of upstanding curls in front. The later and perhaps better-known wig called a full-bottomed wig was more general; this was divided into three masses, one over each shoulder and one at the back. An example of this will be seen in Fig. 91 A and B.

Fig. 88 A shows the slightly shaped coat, with huge cuffs and long waistcoat, which was generally in favour in 1685.

In contrast, Fig. 90 B and C show the shaped waist and full split skirts of five years later. Breeches were no longer visible below these long skirts and the stockings, tied above the knee, covered what little might otherwise have shown. The long waistcoat sleeve fashionable for several years appears beneath the great cuff in Fig. 91. Muffs were worn at the waist, and hats were carried, their necessity as a head-covering being mitigated by the introduction of the large full-bottomed wigs worn by all fashionable gentlemen.

Fig. 90. − 1689

Among the more excessive fashions just before the turn of the century was the shoe with scarlet heel some 2 or 3 inches high and long tongues or flaps rising from the instep of the shoe to several inches up the front of the shin (Figs 90 B and 91 B). The height of the heel made it necessary for the elegant man-about-town to carry a long walking stick in order to walk with any degree of security. This was quite a short-lived fashion and within a few years the flat-heeled shoe with a very large buckle on the instep had taken its place and remained in favour until another short craze for very high heels during the 70's. Coloured hose, particularly red and blue, were much in demand.

One of the most specatacular innovations in the history of English costume arrived in the streets of London during the year 1709. This was the hooped petticoat of enormous proportions (Fig. 92). If we are to believe the writers of the day its circumference was something over 16 yards and Addison in *The Tatler* of 5 June, 1710, tells us that

A

B

1698   1716

Fig. 91

it was 24 yards. Certainly the early illustrations give us the impression that it was both unwieldy and destructive; not only did it take up a large area of space in the streets and ballrooms but also a vast amount of print – for criticism of its fantastic size called forth abuse and satire from practically everyone who could set pen to paper.

However, these gigantic circular hoops did not last long in favour, and a flattened hoop, wide at the sides only, was observed first in 1714. A variety of experiments in hoops of all sizes and shapes occu-

A   B

Fig. 92. – 1720

Fig. 93. – 1720

pied the minds of the fashion conscious for the following half century. Museums all over the country have an interesting and varied collection of such hoops fashioned from wire (resembling watch spring wire), whalebone and horsehair woven into springy, resilient pads; those made from wicker and wood and even hinged metal were rarer but can still be found. Designs ingenious and absurd continued to hold out the petticoats of all those interested in fashion.

As the hooped petticoat appeared, the tall headdress disappeared and a minute bonnet took its place (Fig. 93 A, B and C). The hair was tucked away neatly and a fine forehead was of more account than a multitude of curls. The *Spectator* of 1711 made the following comment on the new silhouette: 'At present the whole sex is in a manner dwarfed and shrunk into a race of beauties that seem almost another species. I remember several ladies who were once near seven foot high that at present want some inches of five' (Figs 92 and 93).

Stays of intricate pattern, laced both front and back, varied very little for the first three-quarters of the century. They were incredibly stiffly boned all over and had an extra stiffening in the front which held the body rigid from waist to breasts; because of this pressure they tended to force up the breasts so that throughout this time those of modest inclination covered their necks and shoulders with a fichu or necklace (Fig. 92). The necklace was made from lace and had no connection with the strings of beads that the term means today. Full dress demanded the low bare neck with various lacy devices to give some original character to the wearer. Lace was still of very great importance and value, for few ladies or gentlemen throughout the eighteenth century were to be seen without ruffles at wrist and throat.

The fabrics used during the century were, on the whole, very light in weight. Silks and taffetas, cut velvets of almost transparent weave, satins and fine printed linens were the most popular throughout the reign of the hooped petticoat.

After the side hoops had replaced the circular hoop, there was a basic gown peculiar to the eighteenth century and though this changed in effect several times it retained certain qualities of construction that could serve equally well from 1714 to 1780. Its form was that of an overdress with tightly-fitting bodice and skirts open in the front to display a petticoat to match or a fine quilted one or an embroidered full length apron. The back was shaped so that a centre panel, folded and stitched from neck to waist, contained sufficient material to flare out from waist to hem in unrestricted pleats. The front of the gown fastened over a stomacher or folded across the stays. The skirts were pleated in wide pleats from the back panel to the front opening and often cut away in a deep curve to show off as much of the petticoat as possible. There was a placket hole over each hip through which a lady could both adjust her hoops and get at her pockets which were tied round the waist over the petticoat and under the gown (Fig. 94). Sometimes the skirts were tucked up by the simple process of pulling the hem through the placket hole: sometimes they were arranged in a more careful manner by a strong thread made in a large loop sewn on the inside of the waist which was brought round the skirts and buttoned on to minute buttons sewn either side of the loose back panel. Thus the 'bunched up' effect, seen in so many paintings of the mid-eighteenth century, was achieved.

The 'sac' backed gown was in a sense a natural development from the panel form. A peculiarly elegant style that fitted the body in the front and fell away in deep pleats from shoulder to hem at the back

Fig. 94. – 1740

(two widths of material were folded into the back forming a graceful train although the sides of the gown could accommodate hoops of any size). With full dress the sides were pleated in a variety of ways so that the largest possible side hoops could be worn (Fig. 94).

As long as the large hoops remained in fashion a vast variety of little waistcoats with elbow-length sleeves, full-skirted jackets and laced bodices were worn. These were just as useful with or without

Fig. 95. – 1740–5

a hoop and for informal wear could be worn over a quilted petticoat. Undress was of great importance to a lady of fashion for it was possible to thus discard both hoops and stays.

As the hoop was the most noticeable innovation for the ladies of the eighteenth century so was the white wig for the gentlemen, and its first appearance was also during the first decade of the century. Presumably the fashion for the immense full-bottomed wig died hard with the older generation for as late as 1730 we still see portraits of elderly gentlemen wearing them. John Gay tells us that

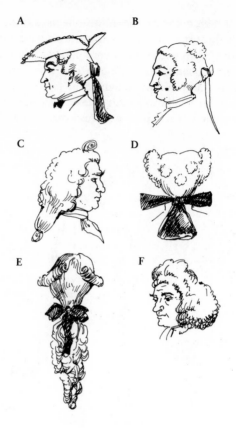

Fig. 96. – 1725–60

'the full-bottom formally combed all before denotes the lawyer and the politician; the smart tie-wig with the black ribbon shows a man of fierceness of temper (Fig. 96 A); and he that burdens himself with a superfluity of white hair which flows down his back and mantles in waving curls over the shoulders, is generally observed to be less curious in the furniture of the inward recesses of his skull' (Fig. 96 E).

Within some five years of the introduction of the small wig there were a dozen or more styles to choose from and barbers vied with each other to produce some fashion more absurd than the last. Many of these fashions were drawn by Bernard Lens in 1725–6 (Victoria and Albert Museum, Print Room, Fig. 96 A, B, C and D) and from this date to the end of the century powdered wigs were still worn.

Presumably the idea came from a superficial knowledge of Classics and it could have been an outcome of the Grand Tour when all young gentlemen went to Italy as part of their education. Certainly some of the late Roman sculptured heads give the impression of queues and tied back hair.

As the ladies' skirts expanded in size the elegant gentlemen's skirts took on a competing outline (Fig. 95 A, B, C and E). Small springs and even foxes' tails were put under the pleats at the sides of the coats so that the skirts almost assumed the quality of those of a nineteenth-century ballet dancer. The waistcoats were sometimes worn with long sleeves, the cuff turned back over the wide cuff of the coat; they were worn indoors and without the coat for informal occasions as the coats were both fragile and costly. One can say the same of wigs for this was the time when nightcaps and turbans took the place of the wig in the privacy of one's own home. By 1740 the now tightly-fitting knee-breeches were brought down over the knee and either fastened with a buckle or buttons just below the knee. Almost as soon as this fashion was introduced the waistcoats lost their sleeves and gradually began to shorten, a process that continued year by year until the 80's when they barely reached the waist. Characteristic of the first half century was the dependence on the waistcoat to cover the shirt. The coat itself rarely had functional buttons for these would have damaged the swing and cut of the garment. Coats were made to be left open to display the elegant features of an even more decorative waistcoat; neither did these coats have collars for the neckcloth or cravat was to be displayed to its uttermost.

Those of more modest means and country gentlemen followed the fashion only as it suited their pockets. There were, of course, a great many sensible woollen fabrics to be had and the frock-coat, which could button up in front, was a useful top coat for all occasions, whilst the waistcoat remained the normal wear for servants and workmen.

It is in 1754 that we first find the reference to 'a gown worn without hoops which was made for them', for in a letter to her daughter Mrs Delaney wrote: '. . . Yesterday after chapel the Duchess brought home Lady Coventry to feast me, and a feast she was! She is a fine figure and vastly handsome. . . . Her dress was a black silk sack, made for a large hoop, which she wore without any, and it trailed a yard on the ground; she had on a cobweb-laced handkerchief, a pink satin long cloke, lined with ermine, mixed with

Fig. 97. – 1755

squirrel skins; on her head a French cap that just covered the top of her head, of blond [lace] and stood in the form of a butterfly with its wings not quite extended, frilled sort of lappets crossed under her chin, and tied with pink and green ribbon – a headdress that would have charmed a shepherd. . . .' From that date on there was an enchanting variety of experiments with the skirts of the gowns and new gowns were made to give something of the same effect (Fig. 99). However, full dress and gowns worn at court, in England at least, continued to have hoops until the nineteenth century.

Throughout the 50's there was an increasing interest in something considered pastoral, the milkmaid hat, tiny shoulder capes with hoods (Fig. 97), the tucked-up petticoats, aprons and fichus, bonnets and mobs. The mob cap itself was a bonnet which fitted the back of the head and carried elegant little frills round the face. It was not yet the grotesque affair worn over the frizzed hair of the 90's (Fig. 92 A and B).

Chapter 7

GEORGE III TO GEORGE IV
1760 to 1820

During the first half of the century brilliance of colour had denoted the gaiety of the young men – the scarlet coat, for instance, had been a great favourite because this could be mistaken for a uniform thus giving the wearer unearned romantic appeal. Now men's clothes as a whole lost something of their flamboyance and even the clothes worn at court tended to moderation in both cut and colour, though not in decoration.

Possibly the change was partly due to the then fashionable colour schemes which demanded a suitably neutral background in order to display the fine embroideries better, mostly of a floral nature, that rambled down the facings, round the cuffs, across the pockets of the coats and all over the waistcoats.

The new cut-away coat fronts not only showed the elegance of the satin waistcoats with their lovely designs but also displayed the tightly-fitting knee-breeches far more than had been the case earlier.

Colours tended towards mouse and mole – even 'dark mouse' and 'pinkish mouse' – soft heather tones and dull greens. Realism in floral decoration could then be achieved against a suitable background.

Buttons of every conceivable substance were used, many of them being made from semi-precious stones, silver, gold and even diamonds.

Although the fashions changed completely before the close of the century Court Dress remained much the same.

Fig. 98. — 1765

Fig. 98 shows all the new tendencies towards the men's fashions of the next decade. The cut-away coat-tails, longer sleeves, and the addition of a collar to the coat, the shorter waistcoat of simpler design, the knee-breeches worn outside the stockings and different shoes – all these things became exaggerated as the century advanced.

With the late 60's came one of the most startling adventures in the mode of hairdressing ever indulged in in this country. This was the high powdered wig, so dear to the heart of fancy-costumiers of future years.

The first inclinations towards higher headdressing was about 1760 when the powdered natural hair was dressed on top of the head instead of at the back, and by about 1765 a slight pad was added to give height to the hair over the forehead. By 1770 the fashion had become an established idea, to be enlarged upon and carried to perfectly ludicrous heights – most absurd between 1770 and 1780. No verbal description can adequately explain the arrangements of these headdresses, but by the careful study of the examples given here some idea of their construction and arrangement can be gained. The natural hair was superimposed by the addition of false curls and switches, the whole padded with wool and horsehair and laid over a wire frame. In its final stages of dressing it was liberally smeared with pomatum and then powdered. The addition of various feathers and ribbons and bunches of flowers, or pearls, was quite usual for daily wear, the evening-dress etceteras being even more ornate; these took the shape of ships in full sail, coaches, windmills, and various other unsuitable items that typified the advancement of civilization in the mechanical world.

As these head-tyrings took such a long time to arrange, the habit of leaving them as a more or less permanent fixture led to the discovery of mice and other less pleasant inhabitants when they were eventually 'undone'!! A huge cap was worn over them at night to keep them in position, so that the next morning only a judicious application of powder and perfume was necessary.

With the grotesque exaggeration of the head the simpler style of dress of the 40's and 50's was enlarged upon and decorated; skirts became increasingly short, the ankle often being visible in the late 70's. And the general tendency to over-ornamentation led to layers of pleated frills on the skirts (Figs 102, 103 A and 104 B). The over-skirt was nearly always decorated at the edges with ruching, lace or a pleated frill, and bunched and puffed with bows of ribbon; sometimes these bunched over-skirts were stuffed with paper (Fig.

Fig. 99. – 1760–70

104 B) to add to their width, and cause a pleasing rustle in movement.

One curious detail will be noticed in Fig. 102 in the style of the child's dress, a simplicity and cut which was to be fashionable some fifteen years later for the adult. Whether the clothes worn by the child in 1775 so appealed to the wearers that the same style was readopted when they reached the age of maturity and selection, is a debatable point, but nevertheless both the long trousers for small boys and the high-waisted and sash-tied dresses for girls of the late 70's make their appearance again as established modes in the late 90's.

Fig. 100. – 1776

The hoop or farthingale, as a wire structure, disappeared in 1780, but the skirts became hardly less full for some five years; pads were worn at the waist, and the addition of flounced and stuffed over-skirts and aprons made up in bulk what they lacked in whalebone support (Fig. 104 B). Waists were considerably higher during the 80's, and the corset, which was still in use, was made higher, once more pushing the breasts up and forming a ridge several inches higher than nature intended. This fashion lasted to the end of the century, though a somewhat more graceful effect was attained during the 90's. Huge bonnets or hats were worn from about 1775 to cover the headdress for morning occasions and going to church. The huge 'picture hats' were not worn till about 1785, when the hairdressing had become more reasonable (Fig. 103 B and C). This new style of hairdressing was strangely similar to that worn some 120 years earlier, cut and curled

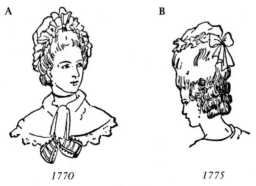

A   B

1770   1775

Fig. 101

Fig. 102. – 1775

so that it stood out either side of the face, giving width but little height. Powder was not used generally after 1785 except for very formal occasions.

An entirely new style asserted itself about this date. This was a sort of pseudo-Greek or Classic style and was carried to extremes in France during the closing years of the century, where a practically transparent garment was worn tied high under the breasts, and the hair cut short to be arranged in a riot of somewhat untidy curls. The new clinging lines raised an agony of reproach from contemporary moralists, but this did not deter its ultimate adoption in this country at about 1800. During the last five years of the 90's the tendency towards a new simplicity, and pastoral habits became more marked.

1782   1788

Fig. 103

The untidy curly hair, huge mob-caps, big shady hats, heelless shoes and high-waisted gathered skirts, complete with sash and fichu, must have appeared amazingly plain and simple after the frivolous absurdities of the 70's and 80's.

The general tendencies already described in men's clothes became increasingly marked. The cuff diminished in size until by 1780 it had entirely disappeared, and in its place a band or buttons finished the sleeve. The frilled shirt-cuffs likewise shrank beneath the lengthening sleeve until merely an inch or so was visible. The collar increased in size until 1780 (Fig. 104 A), when it frequently stood up to the ears. The waistcoat of 1760–70 was still often embroidered, but a general passion for quilting and stripes soon replaced the older embroidered waistcoat. This shrank in size throughout the period, and by 1780 (Fig. 104 A) the waistcoat pocket had been sacrificed in the name of fashion and 'fobs' hanging beneath the short waistcoat were the mode.

Throughout the decade when women wore their hair in the ridiculous powdered and raised style, men imitated them, in as far

A   B

Fig. 104. – 1780

as they were permitted, by the raising of the wig either just in front
(Fig. 106) or all over (Fig. 105), and, by the judicious arrangement
of the side curls, attained in some measure a similar effect as that
worn in less extreme fashion by the ladies.

Those who adopted the extreme styles, called Macaronis, wore
an absurd little tricorn hat on top of the wig, striped stockings and
waistcoat and cut-away coats, and assumed a feminine languor
and an addiction to perfume and snuff. The high-heeled shoes had
large paste or diamond buckles, but otherwise the extremes tended
not towards gaudy ornaments, but rather relied upon cut and fit to
emphasize the extravagances.

Wigs were in a great measure dispensed with during the 80's.
Those who still clung to them wore them small and arranged in two
rows of curls with a small curl at the back. The natural hair cut to

the lobe of the ear once again was the most usual manner of hairdressing.

The masculine silhouette of 1790 varied in every essential from that of 1760. The full skirts, big cuffs, powdered wigs and tricorn hats had been replaced by a cut-away coat, waist-length waist-coat, tight-fitting sleeves, natural hair and hats varying in shape, the most popular styles being those shown in Fig. 107 A, B and C.

The panniers and hooped skirts had

Fig. 105. – 1770

Fig. 106. – 1775

vanished with their various et-ceteras, to be replaced by a high-waisted gown, with skirts less liberal than had been seen for over a century. From the 1790's fashion-plates were introduced in this country, and from that time to the present day fashions changed with a lightning rapidity never before realized. Dozens of minor garments such as short capes and

1790

1795

Fig. 107

coats, fur tippets, scarves, shawls, pelisses, etc., were adopted, altering the standardized styles in a bewildering manner. Curled ostrich feathers as a means of hair decoration and hat trimming were increasingly worn during the 90's, the hair often being dressed by

the addition of a 'bandeau' with feathers stuck into it in the front. The mob-cap was not often seen in England after 1790, the pseudo-Greek style for dressing the hair with ribbons and bands having entirely usurped the rage for the pseudo-pastoral.

About 1808 a turban for evening wear became popular; these turbans for the first few years after

Fig. 108. – 1781   their introduction were quite in the Turkish style, but later they assumed gigantic proportions, and during the early 30's resembled nothing less than a huge cushion.

In Fig. 107 D the earliest form of pokebonnet can be seen. This charming fashion first made its appearance on the disappearance of the dressed 'heads', and was worn with slight modifications and exaggerations for some fifty years.

From 1798 to 1809 one fundamental item in women's clothing was remarkable for its absence; this was the corset. With the coming of the simple clinging little dresses of the French Directoire, literally everything was abandoned which had previously seemed to enhance a lady's charms. It was as complete a revolution from one extreme to another as could be possible.

Hair, heels, jewellery, cosmetics, petticoats and corsets – all were ruthlessly discarded in an endeavour to assume a natural simplicity – possibly a trifle too natural, especially in the case of the rather voluptuous French figures!

Before 1800 the long clinging lines of the French Empire styles had been established in England, and for street wear the dresses and coats were figure-fitting – a style which must have appeared indecently revealing to a generation brought up in farthingales and frills. The closely cut hair, too, was in direct contrast to the curls and fizz of a decade ago. For nearly ten years the style for a simple high-waisted garment of almost transparent consistency formed the foundation for every ensemble. But this was too daring a fashion to retain its original simplicity for long, and about 1802 the usual arrangement was to supplement the dress with a pelisse or tunic, cut on similar lines but only reaching to mid-thigh or knees (Figs 109 B and 110). This pelisse could be decorated in any way; sometimes it was split up the front and the sides embroidered, sometimes the hem was cut to points at the back only or back and front, the sleeves might be long or short and the neck high or low, in fact almost any style could be fashionable so long as it was high-waisted and not below the knees.

When the tunic was not worn, another way of disguising a too-daring transparency was devised by the addition of an apron-front. This was made of the same material as the dress, and sewn on just below the breasts at the 'waist'-line, falling to within a few inches of the hem of the skirt. It was usually decorated in some way, either with embroidery all round the sides and hem, or rows of cord or ribbon.

Short coats varying in length were often worn even indoors (Fig. 109 C) as a protection from cold, as throughout this decade no heavy materials were used except for the outdoor coats. These were invariably trimmed with fur (Fig. 109 A) and practically always had a deep collar or cape covering the shoulders.

Fig. 109. – 1803

Evening dress was even more classic in design. Simple patterns, like the Greek-key, adorned the edges of the over-gown (the two skirts still being fashionable for evening wear until about 1815). The hair, after about 1805, was often in the growing stages, and could easily be tied in a Clytie knot (Fig. 113 C), or, if longer, was worn with a circular plait high up at the back of the head (Fig. 111).

The true classic style was somewhat spoilt by the injudicious addition of pieces of lace and artificial flowers. Nevertheless, a charming effect of simplicity was attained, unrivalled by any other period in history, with the possible exception of the late twelfth century. Simplicity, unfortunately, is the one fashion which has the shortest popularity, and all too soon this was spoiled by the unwarranted addition of a dozen knick-knacks and gew-gaws, and a shorter and fuller skirt soon replaced the flowing classic lines of the opening years of the century.

The fashions retained much of their charm until the 20's. The waist-line was at its highest about 1815 (Fig. 112), and after that date very gradually slid down to normal, over a period of some ten years. A military style — reflection of the Napoleonic Wars — was adopted and found favour for some five years. Braid, frogs, brass buttons, epaulets, high masculine neckwear and tall brimless hats slightly reminiscent of the French soldiers' hats, but rather more decorated (Fig. 113 A), were worn for several years between 1815 and 1820.

Fig. 113 B and C show the manner in which the hair was often cut during the first fifteen years of the century, and later during its growing period was tied up on top with the curls hanging down; this tendency towards a higher hairdressing was to be carried to absurd heights during the following decade.

Little handbags called reticules were adopted as a means of carrying the odds and ends so necessary to a lady's requirements, the pocket which had been previously concealed amidst voluminous skirts having been abandoned with the too-clinging demands of fashion.

Amongst other noteworthy details of the 1810–20 decade, was a new phase in the use of starch on collars, cuffs and the new net over-skirts and frills, a tendency towards ruffles and ruching at neck and wrist, puffed and bunched sleeves (Fig. 114) and a distinct added interest at the hems of the dresses. Also plaids and deeper colourings for practically all the day dresses.

With men's clothes the speed of change was slowing down except in one item — the introduction, or rather establishment, of trousers.

A   B

Fig. 110. – 1811

Fig. 111. — 1807

1815

1820

Fig. 112. – 1815   Fig. 113

These had, as has already been mentioned, been worn for some twenty years by small boys and sailors, but by 1805 they had definitely succeeded the knee-breeches in ordinary attire.

During the early years of the century they were made almost skin-tight (Fig. 116), and the Wellington boot was usually worn over them for walking as well as riding. For evening wear they reached only just below the calf. The fashionable ones were so tight that they were sometimes made of buckskin, and sitting down comfortably was an impossibility.

Ornamentation of the pockets was usual, and the waistcoat was so short that it barely reached the waist. The coat was being cut shorter in front each year from 1795 to 1808. The dimensions eventually

Fig. 114. – 1820   *Fig. 115. – 1798*

arrived at in 1808 are those almost identical with the modern tail-coat.

The passion for revers, started some time before 1790, was en-larged upon and exaggerated, as in the figure illustrated in Fig. 115. The top-hat, ancestor of the one worn today, was established as the general rule for the nineteenth century, about 1805 or earlier. As the tricorn was typical of the eighteenth so the top-hat was for the nineteenth; it is rather a depressing thought that the homburg looks rather as if it may be for the twentieth.

Shirts had abandoned their frilled cuffs, but a double row of frills

Fig. 116. – 1810

was worn down the front, protruding through the V at the top of the abbreviated waistcoat. The neckcloths or cravats were worn even wider than they had been and usually finished in a great knot in front, the sides of the collar underneath standing up to the lobe of the ear.

By 1810 the very short waistcoat had been supplanted in favour of one several inches longer, and the exceedingly tight trousers had taken on a looser, less-fitting appearance, except in the case of evening-dress when they retained their tight-like qualities for several years.

Chapter 8

GEORGE IV, WILLIAM IV AND VICTORIA–1820 to 1850

From 1820 to the present day, ladies' fashions, with the help of tailors and dressmakers with an eye for business, change their shapes and sizes at such a bewildering speed that it is almost hopeless to deal with more than one decade at a time.

The 1820's, then, show us obvious changes – the widened shoulder, leg-of-mutton sleeves, fuller skirts and big hats. During the first five years of this decade the skirts were long, sweeping the ground in some instances, but curiously, in contrast to other periods, the evening dress remained shorter, well above the ankle. This fashion was of course more practical and facilitated dancing, but it is a curious exception to the general rule that seems to have governed every other mode in evening wear. By 1825 the order of things was reversed and the evening dress touched the ground evenly all round, whilst the day dress rose to above the ankle, showing the new boots, never before worn by ladies. The hem of the dress always received the maximum of attention; bands of heavy fur, ruching, or stuffed rolls of material, any trimming in fact that would be sufficiently stiff to hold the skirts out and form a minimum of folds from waist to hem (Fig. 117). After 1828, and as the skirts grew shorter, the creaseless appearance was not so fashionable; often they were gathered into a band at the waist and with this fashion the waist became increasingly small until an hour-glass figure was attained. Very high collars or ruffles were worn in the daytime in contrast to the very low off the shoulder-line adopted for evening wear. Hats and bonnets steadily increased in size during this decade. Some of them were quite charming

Fig. 117. – 1825

until as late as 1826, but after that date they became positively grotesque in shape and absurd in their lavish over-ornamentation (Figs 118 and 119 A). Ribbons and feathers were stuck about with a complete disregard for design. Great mountains of lace and positive flower gardens covered the crowns and if the brims were made of straw, bits and pieces of the ornamentation above were pulled through here and there to relieve the monotony of such a monstrous brim.

Sleeves grew larger and larger and were at length extended on wires at the shoulders or helped out with little bolsters. Shawls and cloaks of ornate design were more modish than coats.

Hairdressing changed considerably during this period from about 1820–5, the Clytie knot and the other style already described were still very fashionable for evening wear, usually with the addition of large bunches of flowers. Another style equally fashionable for day or evening wear was to have the hair parted in the middle with curls hanging down each side, the back hair piled high on top of the head. After 1825, as every other item of clothing became exaggerated so did the hairdressing, and women ventured further and further into the fields of absurd fantasy, and by 1828 we may see headdresses almost as high as those of the 1770's. The usual style adopted was that of a wired-up knot or bow of hair, finished with a few ringlets and a profusion of flowers; the front hair was nearly always cut short and curled, forming a heavy, curly fringe over the forehead and ears. Bows of ribbon, stiffened with silver or gold threads, appeared intermingled with the rosebuds and loops of hair (Fig. 121). When this elaborate method of hairdressing was not favoured, gigantic

Fig. 118. – 1827

Fig. 119. – 1830

turbans, also often made of silver-striped gauze and decorated with long flowing ribbons, were the latest thing in evening wear (Fig. 119 B).

The same tendency towards increasing squareness was almost as pronounced in men's clothing as it was in women's. The sleeves of the coat were made very full at the top and gathered on to the shoulder, often with the addition of padding. The trousers were full and padded at the hips, tapering off to a tightness at the ankle achieved by the new method of fastening the bottom with straps under the shoes. These new trousers were called 'Peg-top' trousers and were exceedingly fashionable during the 20's. The added width of shoulder and hips gave the waist an unnatural appearance of slimness, which in some cases was accentuated by the wearing of stays. As the hips grew in size so the tails of the coat had to be cut out to accommodate them, and in the case of dress clothes these were cut separately and sewn on to achieve a more figure-fitting silhouette. Hats were also much larger and varied considerably during this decade. Although the top-hat was the standard motive for practically every shape, it was amazing what a difference could

Fig. 120. – 1825

be obtained by the slight addition of a few inches here and there. Sometimes they were as much as a foot in height, sometimes the crown was of normal dimensions and the brim enlarged and curled upwards at the sides (Fig. 120). It was about 1820 that the cravat was succeeded by a fashion for a sort of stiff collar made of coloured silk and worn over the high white collar. This could be worn with a bow tie or without and seems to have been essentially a fashion for this decade, as a few years later the cravat and bow was once more the usual neckwear.

'The hair is parted on the forehead, and disposed partly in a plaited braid, which forms a diadem round the summit of the head, and partly in a full knot placed quite behind. A cluster of ringlets issue from the knot, which is transpierced by a pearl arrow. The

Fig. 121. – 1832

braid is also entwined with pearls, a single row of which is brought low upon the forehead,' read the contemporary fashion-plate from which Fig. 121 is taken. So much for the simplicity of the 1830's It is hardly credible, in these days of frantic haste, to contemplate any young woman seriously sitting down at her mirror and arranging her hair in this ridiculous fashion ; even if, by some lucky chance, she had sufficient hair to acquire a coiffure of these dimensions, it must have taken hours to arrange – and only a few seconds to destroy.

These extreme fashions happily only lasted until 1834, and were
then replaced by a simple style which lasted with minor modifications for some twenty years or more. This was parted in the middle
and arranged smoothly across the brow, and either done up at the
back or held in a chignon or net behind the ears. Sometimes curls
were worn at the sides; this fashion formed a suitable lining for the
poke-bonnet, now in its most well-remembered styles (Fig. 122).
The wide shoulders did not entirely disappear until about 1837.
From 1830 to that date they assumed gigantic proportions, wire
and whalebone assisting. With the abandonment of the wide shoulders the sleeves received more attention, great puffs from wrist to

Fig. 122. – 1835

elbow, bell-shaped and frilled, but always the fullness at the bottom. And with this style the skirts dropped once more and became increasingly full, helped out with pads, stiffened petticoats, and in 1839 a hoop. The silhouette, from being X-shaped, changed to that of an inverted V or bell; this shape was further emphasized by the increasing use of shawls and scarves and marabout furs. The neck-line, from being high in 1830–5, was cut in a low boat-shape, a fashion which survived in Queen Victoria's Court until her death.

Several small details were noticeable in the general tendency towards a more 'sugary' effeminacy – so typical of Queen Victoria's reign. The craze for rosebuds particularly; these were worn practically everywhere, for every occasion. Round the face inside the bonnet, tucked in the waistband, fichu, or *décolletée* boat-neck; scattered with studied nonchalance all over the skirts of evening dresses, grouped in little posies to be held in the hand at balls, scattered in the hair, adorning little bits of lace and wire that served the purpose of bonnets (Fig. 122 C); embroidered on dresses, shawls, scarves, etc. In fact one may without exaggeration say that the rosebud was the motif for Victorian innocence. The use of other flowers was considered rather exotic and 'racey', and was therefore reserved for the matrons and elderly women.

Men's clothes during the 30's altered little from those worn during the late 20's, except that the wide padded shoulders and hips diminished at about the same date as the women's wide shoulders. Longer hair was fashionable, this nearly always covering the ears, and a sort of fringe or beard was worn round the edge of the chin. The cravat was now sometimes tied in a large knot, the ends tucked down and into the waistcoat instead of being left in a bow at the throat; any coloured cravat might be worn, including plaids and checks. The shirt was often pleated across the chest, somewhat similar to the pleated dress shirts worn today. The ruffled shirts were not nearly so popular as they had been previously. There was a growing tendency towards black in men's clothes, but colours were still worn a great deal and a fashion for check or plaid trousers began about 1838 to last until about 1880. The use of braid and froggings had not entirely disappeared, as will be noticed in Fig. 123. Greatcoats were still very elaborate, having fur collars and coloured linings, and the hats still remained exaggerated. The chimney-pot hat, however, was not seen later than 1840.

The wraps and scarves and shawls of the 30's were succeeded in fashion by several small garments, with a little more definite shaping,

Fig. 123. – 1832

although both shawls and scarves remained in favour for several years.

These newer styles were called various names such as the casaweck, mantelet, visites, etc. The 'visite' was a three-quarter-length coat for afternoon wear, usually trimmed with lace (Fig. 124). The mantelet was a mantle made long at the back with the sides cut up and long pieces hanging down over the front of the dress (Fig. 125). For summer wear these mantelets were often made of lace. The depth at the back varied considerably, sometimes being only the width of the pieces worn over the shoulders in front. The casaweck was a short coat, usually made of padded silk or satin. These styles owed their popularity to the introduction of the crinoline; the skirts were so full and heavy that a long coat was merely unnecessary

Fig. 124. – 1845

weight, the ladies' legs being already too well covered in a bewildering mass of petticoats and pantaloons. But the close-fitting
bodice was not sufficient warmth for the upper part of the lady, so
that a short coat or scarf or mantle became doubly necessary. Furs
were not worn at this time, though velvet trimmed with fur was
exceedingly popular for mantelets and short coats. Capes and cloaks
of brief dimensions were more popular towards the end of the
decade. The bonnet shrank considerably during the 40's and by
1850 slightly altered in shape, the inverted U giving place to a
flattened O. These were still decorated with ribbons and flowers;
but the side view had altered, the brim and crown now forming a
straight line.

With the ever-increasing size of the crinoline skirt, some method

Fig. 125. — 1845

Fig. 126. – 1847

of breaking up so large a surface had to be devised, so that day dresses were often split up the front, showing a panel of different material. Striped, checked or plaid materials were used and the stripes arranged in the opposite directions on the front panel (Fig. 126), and little bows or tiny ornaments placed down the front. With evening gowns the trouble was easier to mitigate. Layers of frills or strips of lace insertion could be used. Or sometimes the whole skirt from waist to hem might be composed of frills some six inches in depth. Elaborate patterns in braid were often employed on heavier materials.

Large straw hats became fashionable during the summer of 1846. These had the small crown and large brim of the eighteenth-century hats, and were tied with ribbons drawn through the brim from the crown. They were not trimmed except with the ribbons, and were in striking contrast to the flowered and laced bonnets worn at the same time.

Practically the only changes in men's attire during the 40's was the increasing looseness of the trousers towards the 50's and a variation in the neckwear. Otherwise the coat and waistcoat remained almost

Fig. 127. – 1848

unchanged. About 1840 the very high collar that had been so fashionable was replaced by one of less restricting dimensions. The cravat gradually disappeared, and a narrow tie took its place. The more elegant young man even went so far as to turn his shirt collar down over the tie, thus giving his neck much greater freedom. Flowered waistcoats were still worn, but a passion for black had almost eliminated the coloured coat. The lapels of the coat were very wide and turned back to below the waist to show as much of the waist-

Fig. 128. – 1854

coat as possible. About 1849–50 the newest styles adopted a lapel of less width, and when the coat was worn closed the buttoning was decidedly higher. The more ornate styles in headgear were not worn by the really fashionable after 1845, the general and established wear being the top-hat.

Chapter 9

VICTORIA—1850 to 1880

Perhaps the most typical feature of the 50's was the passion for heavy materials and dark colours for day wear, in violent contrast to the pastel shades and white for evening.

So general was the craze for white, indeed, that it was considered almost indecent for a young girl to wear anything else. Pink, perhaps, or if she was out of her teens blue, but yellow and green – no. These shades were reserved for those of more mature years.

For street and morning wear dull purples, magentas, plum and violent shades of blue and emerald green were the most fashionable. And the general fashion for stripes and bands of contrasting materials on all garments (Fig. 128) must have made the streets appear amazingly cheerful, even if a trifle crude to modern standards.

Velvet and plush figured very much to the fore during this decade, and the added weight of these materials must have been almost intolerable but for the timely support of the newest thing in crinolines. The giant cage of whalebone and cord of the 1850's was of even more complicated design than the farthingales of the sixteenth and seventeenth centuries and the panniers of the eighteenth, although it had far more suppleness in that the hoops of whalebone could be easily squashed in any direction. The crinoline was entirely separate from the skirts and petticoats, and was discreetly hidden from any chance view by the voluminous frills of four or more petticoats in close proximity.

A peculiar 'novelty' in the way of a veil appeared in the early 50's (Fig. 128). This was a veil with a little runner cord round the brim

Fig. 129. – 1857

so that, should the wearer wish, a string could be pulled and the 'curtains' drawn, concealing the face – a fashion which increased the absurd persistence in making the female figure into an inverted V shape; the waist having been concealed by the addition of a cape, the head and neck was also concealed by the veiled bonnet.

The width of the sleeves increased as the decade advanced, and by 1857 huge cuffs rivalling those worn by the men in the early eighteenth century (Fig. 129), took the place of the more modest sleeve of the late 40's and early 50's. False sleeves of broderie-anglais, Valenciennes lace or hand-embroideries, were usually worn under the huge turned-back cuffs. Ornament was at its boldest, and braidwork and large velvet flowers adorned every garment that was not already frilled and flounced. Evening dresses were extraordinarily overburdened with festoons of flowers and gathered and bunched-up layers of tulle or tarlatan, as much as twenty yards of material being required for quite a simple evening gown.

Several small details appeared to alter the masculine attire, the most obvious being the turned-down collar, high buttoned coat, almost concealing the waistcoat that had for so many years been such an essential feature of men's dress, and the reintroduction of cuffs to the coats. This latter item was an essential feature of the late 50's. Although small turned-back cuffs were sometimes worn as early as 1853, by 1855 they were essential to the well-dressed man, but had entirely disappeared soon after 1860. Less formal modes were slowly creeping into the wardrobe of those who cared for 'sports' and country life. A straw hat, previously unheard of for men, made its appearance for the seaside and river. This fitted the head in the crown and had a large somewhat soft brim, usually turned up behind. It was about this time that top-hats were abandoned for cricket, and a narrow tie similar to those worn today took the place of the wide ties and cravats of earlier days. The 'full-skirted' and 'tailed' coats were still, however, the only adopted styles; the cutaway coat was a revelation of the 60's.

The year 1860 saw the crinoline in its most exaggerated proportions as a circular skirt – if such an absurdity can be called a skirt. About 1861, a tendency to elongate the back almost to the extent of a train altered the shape considerably, and from being a half-circle, in the side elevation, it became a slowly lengthening isosceles triangle (Fig. 131). By 1866 various experiments were being tried out, including a high-waisted gown with a straight skirt, full at the bottom like an inverted V; the gradual lengthening of the skirt at the back,

Fig. 130. – 1860

however, eventually suggested the new idea. This was to turn the skirt up and fasten it at the waist, in much the same way as the bustles of the seventeenth century, showing the skirt beneath, which now assured the importance of the main skirt. By 1868 the crinoline had been consigned to the rubbish heap and the bustle had usurped its 'throne'. The real circular crinoline, in its last days of popularity, rose well above the ankles of its wearer, displaying to the interested spectator little boots made of coloured silk or cloth with patent toe-caps and striped stockings. When the skirts were not short, an 'improved' crinoline was worn; this was arranged with a complicated series of cords, so that it could be raised or lowered at will. When this stage was reached, it was only too obvious that it could not remain in fashion and increase in size for long, as it had become the source of a hundred jokes and satirical drawings.

In the matter of headdress several new ideas were prevalent during the early 60's, chief of which being the 'pork-pie' hat (Fig. 131 A). This was very fashionable for two or three years, and was usually worn in conjunction with the chignon. Later, about 1864, little hats with brims and decorated with feathers replaced them, and the chignon disappeared in favour of long curls again. Bonnets of lace and ribbon were nearly always worn indoors, and the outdoor bonnet diminished in size until it was merely an excuse for a tiny brim and lots of ribbons, flowers and feathers tied under the chin (Fig. 131 B and C). The deep rich colourings of the 50's were succeeded for a few years by darker, more sombre tones, but about 1867 contrasts of a very vivid sort asserted themselves again; purple and yellow, and magenta and royal blue being two very favourite combinations.

Both long magyar coats and short-waisted coats were very popular, and a new style in capes was seen in 1865. This was cut with a tight-fitting yoke over the shoulders, and the fullness gathered in equally all round instead of being shaped on the cross as had previously been the case. Fringes and feathers became popular as an adornment for evening dress and pleated or gathered frills of varying widths almost always appeared on the skirts as long as the crinoline was worn. The earlier edition of the 'bustle' seemed to rely on colour contrasts for its decoration more than feathers, flowers and frills, but this was only typical of the years '68 and '69. By 1870 a renewed fervour for wild decoration set in, hardly diminishing throughout the century.

For men the most noticeable innovation of the 60's was the new

Fig. 131. – 1865

sack-coat. This was the forerunner of the modern lounge-suit coat, though in their first stages they were considerably longer than they are today. They were made with three buttons, of which only the top one did up (Fig. 132 B) and were often made of velvet, the edges bound with braid. The typical 'dandy' of the 60's wore 'Dundreary whiskers', loud check trousers and a monocle. The fancy waistcoat disappeared with the abandonment of the long-skirted coat, and was succeeded by one made of the same material as the coat. Another style in coats was the cut-away coat, similar in style to the modern morning coats, curving inwards from a place some three inches below the bottom button.

Hats and caps showed new variety. A flat cap with a little turned-up brim and made of tweed was quite popular during the late 60's and the shortened top-hat (Fig. 132 B) was exceedingly smart. On the whole men's dress became nonchalant again in contrast to the extravagantly elegant styles of a few years earlier. Cut and style in men's clothes, as we know them today, were conspicuous by their absence, and the loose uncreased trousers, and coats that touched the wearer only on the shoulders had almost the informality of pyjamas, and indeed in some contemporary illustrations certainly look as if they'd been slept in. The tie, as we know it today, had definitely established itself as the only form of neckwear over the collar. The collar still varied considerably in size and shape, sometimes stiff and upstanding, or soft and turned down at the front edges only. The back was still rarely seen turned down over the tie. Ties could be knotted and held in place with a pearl pin or solitaire, or tied in a bow. The former style seemed the most popular. Button-holes were much affected and cigarette-smoking became a habit.

With the establishment of the bustle the waist-line descended. At least the shaping of the waist altered not at all, but the actual line where the bodice ended was several inches below the accentuated waist in front, whilst the skirt at the back stood out horizontally from the waist sometimes as much as sixteen inches (Fig. 133).

Such a multitude of odd frills, ribbons and flounces adorned these skirts that it is exceedingly difficult to give any comprehensive description. Sometimes the back of the bodice came down, forming a sharp curve at the back and spreading out over the bustle fan-wise. The skirts could be either split up the back or front, or gathered at each side, and the front part dragged up in a series of U-shaped folds and the back part bunched up over the bustle. When the skirt was split at the back a train or cascade of frills usually covered the back

Fig. 132 A. – 1855   Fig. 132 B. – 1869

of the under-skirt. The split edges of the over-skirt could be ornamented in any manner, but usually a gathered or ruched frill was
sewn on to the border, the sides being drawn up to make as much
of the frilling as possible (Fig. 136 B).

In 1875 the bustle started to diminish. The angle from the back
of the waist was succeeded by a figure-fitting shaping over the hips.
During the years 1877 and 1878 the flatness tended to be so exaggerated that in some cases the fullness of the skirts did not begin till
the knees. 1878 and 1879 witnessed another experimental stage,
with what was then called the fish-tail skirt, tight-fitting to a few
inches above the ankle. With these dresses an ankle-chain was worn
to stop the wearer from taking too large a step and thus splitting her
very restricting garments. These dresses were worn several inches off
the ground and are in direct contrast to the bustles which preceded
and succeeded them, so short a period indeed that many records
miss it altogether, merely noting the temporary rise and fall of the
bustle towards the 80's. It is a particularly interesting style in its
extreme brevity of popularity and in the peculiar fact that those
really fashionable ladies who adopted it in its most restricting forms
wore a single garment underneath composed of chamois leather
figure-fitting to the ankles, and allowing the knees only an inch or
two's play. Stripes and plaids were the most fashionable materials
for these dresses, and little jackets with a stiffened basque were worn
with them (Fig. 135). The only tendency towards the bustle was a
flat bow at the back and often even this distinction was not evident.

During the early 70's the hair was generally worn in long curls
down the back, whilst the front was drawn off the face and ears,
showing to full advantage the large gaudy ear-rings so dear to the
hearts of the late Victorians.

Later it was piled higher at the back in a sort of 'bun' with the
curls hanging from the protuberance. Another style fashionable in
the middle of the decade was that of tying the hair in a huge loose
knot. (Fig. 136 B). All sorts of variations arrived about 1877, a complicated combination of chignons, curls and plaits being very popular
(Fig. 134). The closing years of the decade saw the hair done up
rather high at the back of the head and curls were reserved for
evening wear only.

Little hats and bonnets were typical from 1870 to 1880, and in
a variety so large that several pages of drawings would be inadequate
description. During the first five years the hats were definitely
perched on the front of the head, and never had a brim more than

Fig. 133. — 1874   Fig. 134. — 1877

Fig. 135. – 1878

an inch or two in width. Crowns were negligible for the most part, but some of them tended to height. They were all decorated lavishly with flowers, feathers, lace or ribbons, and an absurdity called a bonnet was worn (Fig. 136 A). This resembled more than anything the lace glass mat of a more elegant 'luncheon set', and was tied beneath the chin with a wide ribbon. Occasionally a tiny feather or a bow of ribbon of microscopic dimensions adorned the 'bonnet'. Contemporary ridicule termed it 'a postage stamp and a pair of boot-laces'. This bonnet was rarely seen, except worn by old ladies, later than 1877. After 1875 the angle inclined more to the back of the head and the crowns became higher, but still with a minimum of brim.

Men's styles changed hardly at all, except for the complete abandonment of the old fashions in preference for the sack-coat,

A   B

Fig. 136. – 1873

and still further adventures in the way of hats. These included the deer-stalker's hat with the little bow on top, a sort of sporting cap made rather similar only without the 'ear-flap', and a round-crowned hard hat, ancestor to the bowler of later years. Striped and checked trousers were still the latest thing, and great-coats of loud check patterns were very fashionable. The Dundreary whiskers remained in favour throughout the decade, sometimes being worn without a moustache, and in some cases with the addition of a tiny pointed beard on the chin. The hair was still worn rather long and brushed forward over the ears at the sides.

Chapter 10

VICTORIA TO EDWARD VII
1880 to 1901

The first three years of this decade re-adopted the same tendency to elongate the waist that had been the vogue before the advent of the short-lived 'fish-tail'. The dresses worn 1880–3 were almost exact replicas of those worn 1875–7, the only substantial difference being that the earlier gowns had trains whilst these barely touched the ground – except in the case of evening gowns. There was a marked attempt at simplicity in the top part of the dress – high collars, tight sleeves, and a general 'fit' that adhered in every essential to the corset (Fig. 137). The draped skirt was now called a 'fish-wife' and was often terminated with a fringe, or made of contrasting material to the rest of the gown. The mixture of two plaids of entirely different colours was very popular. The year 1881 saw the bustle once more established; indeed, fashions seemed to be advancing backwards. During this decade the fashions of 1885 resembled their prototypes of 1875 in almost every detail except length, for the latter were considerably shorter.

The fastenings of the bodice were now always in front, whereas a decade earlier they had been at the back, and the collar was worn practically always up to the throat.

Hats were larger and for a year or two favoured a brim, and, of course, the hairdressing had changed. The hairdressing of the 80's was somewhat dull and uninspired, merely being lumped up on top of the head to begin with, and later scraped tightly up at the back with all the hair piled well over the forehead (Fig. 138 A). This high hairdressing was often helped out with the aid of pads, and the

Fig. 137. – 1882

Fig. 138. — 1888

hats had necessarily to become much taller in the crown to accommodate the hair (Fig. 138 B). One rather startlingly new fashion appeared for evening wear – this was the sleeveless gown. It was considered extremely advanced and rather naughty, although in reality it only exposed the shoulder and about four or five inches of arm between the draped fichu and the long gloves, which were an essential part of the evening wear. Little shoulder capes, fur-trimmed, were worn to cope with this newly exposed part, and prevent chills from draughts. Trains were still worn on evening gowns, but they could be lifted and worn over the arm should their wearer require to join in the exceedingly exhausting occupation of dancing. There were, also, at the same time dresses that followed the day fashions in length and were about two or three inches from the ground – for those who took dancing more seriously.

New interests in sports, such as tennis and bicycling, tended to make the men's clothes even more informal than previously, and during the 80's we even see tweed knickerbockers, and knee-breeches frequently adopted in preference to trousers. The trousers had been the only shape of nether-garment worn by men for eighty years. But now (after about 1889) for all sporting events the Norfolk jacket and knee-breeches take the board (Fig. 139 A). The Norfolk jacket was in every way an entirely new idea, no belted coats having been worn since the time of William and Mary. And the increasing use of tweeds for men's clothes became an established medium about the same date, when previously it had been looked upon in rather the light of an eccentricity than a rule. Both the straw 'boater' and the bowler-hat owe their origin to the experiments of the 80's, and from that date these two singularly unattractive styles have been constantly in fashion (Fig. 139 B and C).

Men's full evening dress was also established in the early 80's and has done little in the way of advancement since that date, though possibly a little more attention to fit is more evident now than it was fifty years ago!

The top-hat, dark coat and striped trousers still remained the regular town wear and the coat was cut with a slight waist in contrast to the earlier sack-coats; cuffs or imitation cuffs were still worn quite frequently on the coats.

During the year 1891 the bustle once more went out of fashion, to be succeeded by a rather loose-fitting skirt, fuller at the hem and moulded tightly over the hips. From about 1891 to 1893 the skirts trailed the ground, and were supplied with a little fringe of velvet

A

B

C

Fig. 139. – 1890

or plush to catch the dust! With the departure of the bustle, the new interest was centred on the sleeves, and these grew in size and width until 1895, when for a short time they almost exceeded the gigantic sleeves of the 1830's. The general contour, indeed, differed very little from that of 1830, except that the skirts were considerably longer and the hats smaller, though even some of these tended to ridiculous exaggeration in their manner of ornamentation (Fig. 141 B and C). Even the high neck with an Elizabethan ruffle was worn. And the tightly laced waist diminished in size to alarmingly small dimensions: a fourteen- or sixteen-inch waist was fashionable and an eighteen-inch was positively large. The shape of the skirt now flared out evenly all round, 1893 (Fig. 140), and the fashionable outline was sustained by a band, some nine inches wide, of tailor's canvas attached to the inside of the hem. The little fringes were still worn at the edge of the skirt to catch the dust and prevent it penetrating on to the bottom of the dress itself. Heavy materials and rather dull colours were very fashionable – a combination of black and white, and navy blue and nigger brown being considered very smart. It was about this time that brown shoes and stockings replaced the black ones that had been worn for several years. These were only worn in conjunction with a navy-blue suit or dress!

It is rather an interesting fact that in making the bodices of these gowns, the sleeves, being of primary importance, were cut out first, three or four yards of material being required for them alone. The bodice itself was made out of the pieces that were left. These pieces were all quite small and fitted together with the assistance of a tight lining and bones at every seam to produce an entirely creaseless surface. The sleeves were stiffened by a complicated bunching up of tailor's canvas, or in more exaggerated styles by the addition of wires. Usually the part of the sleeve covering the forearm was tight-fitting – these were called 'Leg-of-Mutton' sleeves. But 'Bishop' sleeves were very popular, these being full from shoulder to wrist, and another addition of tailor's canvas was worn at the wrist.

Coats to cover the more exaggerated styles were inconvenient in their excessive weight. Sometimes a short coat was worn with huge sleeves and a little sharply curved-out basque, but generally the cape or cloak were the accepted form of outdoor wear. These were made in various styles, cut on the cross, or gathered into a shoulder-yoke, the smartest being those worn very short and full that only reached to the elbow (Fig. 141 A). Velvet and cloth judiciously mixed were

Fig. 140. – 1893

worn in the winter and lighter ones of lace and crape for the summer. The high collar was always worn.

The high collar was an essential feature of the late 90's, and very few ladies cared to break away from the accepted style for day wear; the 'medici' collar and the straight band were equally popular, whilst the new 'blouses' usually affected a masculine turn-down collar. These blouses were a very new feature of the later 90's and followed the masculine shirt in style, with the exception of the ridiculously

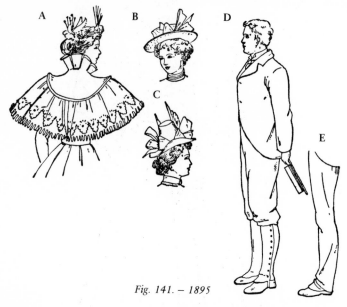

Fig. 141. – 1895

full sleeves. They were worn a great deal by ladies who indulged in the daring pursuit of bicycling and other sports, and usually worn with a neat navy-blue suit.

The high-collar craze was even carried to the extent of being worn with evening dresses, though in this case a wide ribbon, ruffle or band of ruching tied with ribbon was worn round the throat, leaving the chest and shoulders quite often bare. Little boned lace collars, attached to a sort of 'dickey' of lace or net, were worn underneath a bodice that was not cut sufficiently high for the fashionable requirements.

There was no standard rule during the 90's that governed the size of hats. These might be ludicrously small (Figs 140 and 141 A) or exaggeratedly ornamented. As long as they were 'perched' and not worn on the head they were equally fashionable. The hair was dressed a little more informally than it had been during the late 80's. The general tendency was to pile it loosely on top, allowing it to 'puff' slightly all round, especially in front over the forehead.

From 1895 the skirts tended to be fuller at the back again, often sweeping the ground, and the corset was designed to give the figure a different angle. The corset of the 1890–5 era was merely curved sharply inwards, so that the thorax was crushed with a general pressure, the hips and bust bulging above and below. The newer ones produced a flatness in front from the waist downward, and the back sharply curved, so that the hips were thrown backwards and the bust forward. Possibly the easiest way to explain the fashionable figure of the late 90's is to draw a vertical line with an S over it,

Fig. 142. – 1900

slightly tilted backwards; the waist occurs where the S crosses the line (Fig. 142). The waist was still absurdly small, and although the sleeves diminished considerably towards the close of the century, the wasp effect was still maintained, as the upper part of the body was no longer restrained, and tended to bulge over the lowered corset. For those who were less ample-bosomed, 'forms' of buckram were worn, and rows of frilling were sewn on to the undergarments to give the desired voluptuous lines.

Dresses made entirely of 'broderie-anglais' were extremely fashionable in the last years of the century (Fig. 142), and hats tended to width rather than to height, large 'alsatian' bows being one of the chief items of adornment.

Various extraordinary 'suits' of masculine cut and with 'knicker-bockers' were worn by women for bicycling, and the leg exposed as far as the knee was a hitherto unheard-of audacity.

During the 90's men's clothes tended if anything to become even more informal than previously; the 'knickerbockers' had been defi-nitely established for country wear, and these were often worn with gaiters (Fig. 141 D) or spats and 'cycling' stockings. A new type of coat, sharply curved away from the waist and without tails (Fig. 141 D) was equally popular worn with either trousers or knicker-bockers..

Fig. 141 E shows the still uncreased trouser worn crumpled well over the instep and almost covering the heel at the back. The cloth used in the 90's was not usually as thick as the suitings used today, so that the material followed the line of the leg, producing folds at calf, thigh and knee.

Incongruous though these fashions seem to our modern eyes, they were amazingly appropriate for the types that wore them, so typical of the elegant and slightly pompous placidity in which the late Victorians basked.

Chapter 11

EDWARD VII TO
ELIZABETH II—1901 to 1970

The twentieth century began with an extraordinary contrast between the clothes worn by the rich and the poor; at no other time in the history of English costume have there been quite such carefully segregated classes made obvious by the extremes of fashion.

It was indeed an important function in earlier times to see that practical clothes were passed on to the less fortunately placed connexions of any household and even the less practical ones could be handed down with a certain amount of grace and usefulness to poorer relations.

All through the Victorian era there had been a certain decorous attitude against ostentation. It had not been correct to wear bright colours or attract undue attention and the dreadful idea of wearing unrelieved black, as mourning for even remote relations, had tended to make the majority adhere to black and grey as a basic necessity in a community that had large families often riddled with consumption and other incurable illnesses. No sooner were they out of mourning for one relative than they were plunged once again into this dreary uniform. However, such garments could be handed down to one's poor relations or servants and appear perfectly suitable for their needs.

This convention seems to have been swept away with the accession of King Edward, and the rise of a new aristocracy which tended to seek its stimulus from an almost arrogant display of wealth, colour and a sort of hothouse languor, which produced a smart circle more akin to a flock of butterflies than ordinary men and women. Nothing

Fig. 143. – 1903

sensible or practical appeared in the extensive wardrobe of the rich woman though every gown was designed for some particular purpose. No longer could servants find the long trailing cast-offs of their mistresses of the slightest use to them.

All the trappings of fashion were expensive – from the corsets and laced petticoats, fine embroidered underwear, complicated boned linings and interlinings, padding, frills and furbelows (to augment the hips and bust) to the feathers and furs which came from all parts of the world – and cost, even in those days, a small fortune to import and use with the care and trained skill such things require.

These items were only a small part of the whole because the gowns themselves, made from fine silks and satins, broderie anglaise, velvet and fine facecloth, either hand-painted or hand-embroidered, required the services of dressmakers or 'artists' of remarkable ability and skill who understood how to cut and arrange, as fashion demanded the fitted bodices and full-flaring skirts.

All this made the little home-made garment almost pathetic in contrast to the highly sophisticated gowns of the wealthy.

Elegantly corseted ladies with long-handled parasols and over-trimmed hats – bearing flowers, fruit and feathers, of an enormous size – with marabou or feather boas round their lace-collared necks, trailing skirts which, when lifted from the ground, displayed a wealth of frilled petticoats, were a sharp contrast to the bustling working girl with her ankle-length coat and skirt (Fig. 143).

The fashionable corset produced a tiny waist which accentuated both bust and hips and to emphasize the bust, tucks and frills, braids and laces decorated the bodice and helped to accentuate the then fashionable, boned, lace neckpiece – boned right up to the ears to make the neck look longer. Young girls were bribed, coaxed and bullied at an early age into tight corseting so that on their coming out into polite society they might appear with something approaching an eighteen-inch waist.

Every occasion demanded a separate outfit and the fashion magazines, which were just beginning to circulate in some considerable number, displayed such garments as Breakfast Gowns, Tea Gowns, Matinée Gowns, Afternoon and Evening Gowns, Dinner Gowns, Ball Gowns, Walking Dresses, Travelling Coats, Dust Coats (for motoring) (Fig. 145 A), Bicycling Habits, Sports Suits (individually suited for such pastimes as shooting, hunting and fishing as well as yachting, golf and tennis) and a host of other 'suitable' changes for a lady of leisure.

The main difference between a gown and a dress at this time was that a gown was required to sweep the ground and could be held up by a clip attached to the wrist or waist if necessary; a dress was designed for some form of exercise and, therefore, made short enough to clear the ground when walking. A walking dress might be made of some fine facecloth or serge. Any type of outside sports (with the exception of tennis) required the services of a tailor skilled

Fig. 144. – 1910

in the practicalities of tweeds and the various fabrics normally used for men's wear.

Most of the day 'gowns', which were in some way similar to a decorative housecoat, were made from flimsy, frothy materials, broderie anglaise, lace or some vaguely transparent fabric decorated with more lace, ribbons, swansdown or marabou. Their purpose normally was to give a sense of exotic undress should the wearer want to dispense with her all too tight corset and still look charming enough to play the hostess.

The suitability of most of the various types of dress for the occasion to which they were dedicated did not lie in their specific cut nor in the actual fabrics chosen for their make-up; rather was their purpose indicated by some decorative motif. Thus a bathing or yachting costume might have a sailor collar, a shooting outfit be decorated with leather straps and buckles, a bicycling habit have the austerity of a mannish coat and baggy knee-breeches.

The evening gowns were usually cut low to reveal white shoulders and swelling bosoms in contrast to the high necks worn during the day time; often sleeves were worn with evening dress but these began off the shoulder and rarely covered the elbow unless with a fall of lace. Long gloves were essential and a fan a necessity to keep the air flowing in the stuffy atmosphere of a ballroom.

The artificial atmosphere engendered by the full-sweeping garments and tiny waists was completely in keeping with the fashionable ideology of the time. Reality had no place in polite society.

Those who could not afford the endless variety of suitably designed garments for every separate occasion wore a suit with full ankle-length skirt, a blouse with a high boned lace collar or a masculine collar and tie, and a straw boater or tam o'shanter (for sports) or something more ornate in the way of headdress for some more formal occasion. Such skirts were tightly buckled at the waist with a wide belt and an ornamental clasp.

Men's formal wear still included the frock coat with its full skirts, often worn with a coloured waistcoat, pin-stripe or checked trousers and, of course, a top-hat (Fig. 145 B).

Morning coats were not necessarily black but were designed in a number of tweeds and small check patterns with trousers of the same material. The edges were often bound. Quoting from the *Tailor and Cutter* of 1906: 'No doubt ribbon as binding wears out easily on the edges much sooner than the cloth edge, but they are easily replaced and give the garments a smart appearance' and again 'Styles in cloth lean towards large checks more or less defined.'

Lounge suits, jackets, blazers and dinner jackets were all made long, reaching at least half way down the thigh.

A variety of men's sports and travelling wear included the travelling Ulster with a shoulder-cape (Fig. 144), usually designed for a large check tweed; a gent's motoring sac with 'panteen' collar; the Norfolk jacket with its broad pleat at the back and a belt above the 'poacher's' pockets; yachting blazer and cap, bicycling breeches and knee-breeches (a variety almost as extensive as that worn by the ladies); deer-stalker hats, soft tweed hats and caps, motoring caps with goggles and a host of other styles in soft headgear.

The bowler hat and the top-hat were reserved for the city and formal wear, though by 1909 the *Tailor and Cutter* pronounced that 'the bowler hat is an abomination to the individualist in head-covering . . . tasteless depravity and follow-my-leader . . . men of individuality eschew it and never give it peg room in their hatstand'.

Fig. 145. – 1910

Trousers were made long enough to conceal the instep but there was no turn-up except for sports wear until about 1912. The centre crease first appeared in about 1907 when it was found easier to keep the trousers looking tidy if they were folded in that manner. By 1914 the male silhouette had changed (Fig. 147) to something not far removed from that of fifty years later. Boots with cloth tops were popular and spats a necessity for the well-dressed business man.

The world in which the Edwardian lived was one far removed from that of today. It is, indeed, doubtful if any generation in history has had to adapt itself so rapidly to a new outlook as the young Edwardian of good family had to with the coming of the First World War. There were certain restless movements towards a new freedom, particularly noticeable in women's dress, in about

A   B

Fig. 146. – 1913

1910. Experimental at first, there was a definite breaking away from the sweeping petticoats and flowing trains towards the hobble skirt, the harem skirt or Jupe Culotte as it was first named.

In 1912 we find two new styles of dress both provoking a storm of indignant criticism (Fig. 146 A and B). These were the Tallien dress, with its skirt split sometimes almost as high as the knee (the idea being that it gave more freedom for dancing the tango which was the latest rage of the time), and the pannier dress, supposedly

inspired by the eighteenth century but bearing little resemblance to
its charming origin.

Numerous and amusing as some of these experiments were, the
really modern trend was towards more masculine suitings; the
suffragette movement was rife and masculine women asserting their
rights in sensible boots, neat serge skirts and high starched collars

Fig. 147. – 1914

were to be seen as often as those who continued to follow the
dictates of fashion.

In 1913 Leon Bakst turned his fertile imagination to dress design
and ballet-length skirts revealed a coy pantalette at the ankle. Corset
advertisements warned the then fashionable world that 'every lady
of fashion in Europe and America now knows it. The waist and
hips are gone, the back is flat, the figure lithe, sinuous and normal.'

So when the War arrived, women were already wearing something more practical and less encumbering although hats of in-

congruous size still appeared for festive occasions. The new idea of cutting the hair short, bobbed and clubbed, as it was then called, tended to make the hatpins obsolete and those advanced women who had cut off their hair found large hats impossible to secure.

Several predominant features of dress occurred during the 1914–18 War. The full, day skirts which flared from waist to hem were nearly always worn with boots (Fig. 148). These frequently had cloth tops and could be fastened with either laces or buttons. The boots were high, covering the calf, and the skirts were short enough to just cover the top of the boots. Furs and feathers were still very much a part of a woman's dress, though the feathers were long and slim, and appeared in the majority of fashionable hats sticking up or down at an angle from the crown. Furs were luxuriant and were used to trim coats and suits as well as being worn as a fur around the neck. Huge muffs were also to be found, often used as a sort of handbag for storing oddments.

Furs were possibly the prerogative of the *nouveau riche* – those who made money from 'munitions' and those who did not necessarily have to take part in the actual warfare or devastation. Wealth covered a variety of sins, sports and pastimes.

It was during the war years that the fashion for powder and lipstick for the handbag began to be a normal necessity. No longer was it necessary to do one's face in the privacy of a bedroom but it could also be retouched on the parade ground as sketches in *Punch* of the time make obvious.

It was also during the 1914–18 War that long dresses, except for evening, vanished – the shorter ones tending to be fuller with perhaps several frills from waist to hem. Waist-lines hovered between high and low, sometimes with an almost Regency slimness, sometimes draped at the hips but more often belted at the waist with a wide belt. The tailored suit which had become almost a uniform during the war years was no longer worn by the really fashionable after the War.

The 'Flapper' had made her appearance during the war period – the name being coined from the teenager's flapping pigtail with immense bows of ribbon on both the head and on the end of the plait. For a few short years it was fashionable for the young girl to wear her hair long, possibly in ringlets (Mary Pickford style) but this fashion did not last after about 1922. From 1918 until 1922 experiment in ladies' clothes was almost as varied as that of the few years that preceded the War. Generally fashion trends tended to

Fig. 148. – 1915

A   B   C

Fig. 149. – 1920

borrow ideas from the Oriental, Egyptian, Red Indian as well as Spanish traditional costumes. The ability to wear a Spanish shawl draped under one arm and over one shoulder and a piled-up Spanish hair 'do' with a large comb was considered the height of sophistication. Curls stuck down to the cheeks and commonly referred to as 'Spit Curls' accompanied this style of evening wear. Fig. 149 B shows a dress designed to imitate the draped shawl.

Tightly fitting evening caps (Fig. 149 A) designed in a vaguely Egyptian style were to be seen at dances and dinner parties as much as the Red Indian styles of beaded headband (possibly decorated with a feather), deeply-fringed tunic dress, slave bangle and, sometimes, even an ankle bracelet. Oriental interests were strictly Chinese and real Chinese Mandarin coats began to be worn as evening wraps while Mandarin and Coolie hats appeared for daytime wear.

The early 20's saw the strange fashion for draping coats. They were not often worn to button up at all but fashionable shapes were very loose and could be draped round the figure in the manner of a cloak. The line to be obtained was loose from the back and held up rather tightly just below the buttocks emphasizing the back of the

Fig. 150. – 1927

thighs. Feathers, beads and fringes were the characteristic decorations of most dressy garments of the decade but a new tendency for large geometric or cubistic patterns in brilliant colours also appeared on almost any item of clothing. The Fair Isle jersey or jumper was typical of this particular tendency (Fig. 150 A).

With the coming of the Charleston in 1924 the dresses were built to swing and the fantastic bead and sequin craze began. Many of these dresses are to be found in museums today, for their workmanship was exquisite. Every bead had to be sewn on separately or the dance floor might become a nightmare of rolling beads. The normal pay for such a chore was 7s. 6d. per dress, possibly one of the most recent examples of cheap sweated labour. A comparatively flat-heeled sandal-type shoe in bright colours was normally worn for dancing because the acrobatics, required from a really skilled dancer of the Charleston could not be performed with high heels.

It is difficult to gain a true version of the fashions of the 20's from the fashion drawings of that time. There existed a cult for exaggeration amongst fashion artists – much the same as that of today – to deform the figure rather than adorn it. The delightful drawings in contemporary *Punch* give us a much better idea of the charm and contrasts to be seen in everyday life, of the slinky little figures, with their skimpy dresses, high heels, ear-rings and Eton crops or shingled heads, displaying a rich variety of uneven hems, cloche hats, draped fur coats and brief, fringed dresses contrasting strangely with their more formal escorts who still tended to stick obstinately to the prescribed attire of their fathers.

We can be justifiably certain of one particular peculiarity throughout the 20's – no lady with any pretence to fashion showed where her waist was. Any possible belt or girdle was worn round the hips. Otherwise, the dress or gown was cleverly cut so that it fell straight from the shoulders to the hips. Underneath the dress was worn a one-piece corselette which was built to flatten the bust, dismiss the waist and hold the hips and thighs in place. Should the wearer naturally own a 'boyish' figure she could display a back open to below the waist. Many of the dresses still in existence are beautifully cut with the back open to the top of the pelvis (Fig. 151).

All the day dresses from about 1920 to 1925 were straight, perhaps with a tabard over them or with a couple of flares in the abbreviated skirt, and sleeveless in summer often with just one shoulder strap for evening. It was perhaps one of the most flagrant changes that fashion has ever provoked, for women born before the

Fig. 151. – 1928

close of the nineteenth century could well remember the corseting –
if not of themselves, of their mothers and sisters – and the high-
boned neckpieces and lacy hats and pinafores which were still worn
just before the War by the teenagers.

Street photographs of this time show that, although the majority
of the bustling crowd were wearing clothes of the 20's, there were a
great many older people in capes and bonnets, long-skirted neat
suits, frock coats and Ulsters, top-hats and morning coats, stiff collars
and spats.

Several changes took place during the last few years of the 20's:
for instance, the perfectly straight line gave place to experiment in
cutting material on the cross, adding flares and gores so that there
was a new sense of movement in both dress and coat (Fig. 153). A
completely circular skirt, attached somewhere at the hipline of

a gown, was normal for day dresses whilst the same experiment on an uneven hipline produced the uneven, flaring skirts for evening wear. Such gowns might touch the ground at the back rising to well above the knee in front. Flimsy, floating fabrics were all the rage, many of them transparent from the knee to the ground (Fig. 154 B).

Beach and house pyjamas were worn and a one-piece trouser suit, which could be stepped into and zipped up at back or side, made its first appearance. Ladies' trousered suitings in linen or tweed were tailored with as much care as those worn by men. It was no longer thought immoral to see a woman wearing trousers, and trousers of one sort or another, had come to stay.

The austerity of the Eton crop and 'shingled' head began to wane towards the end of this decade and hair was once more permitted to grow although the waving process of the time tended to produce intensely stylized coiffures.

Men's clothes began to take on a new look about 1924 when the pull-over started to replace the waistcoat (Fig. 152 A). This could be made with, or without, sleeves and either canary yellow or 'Fair Isle' were the most popular styles. The Fair Isle made a bright spot on every golf course. Knee-breecher suits of tweeds, no longer quiet and restrained in colour or design, appeared in loud checks or plaids with increasingly baggy breeches which gradually got fuller and longer as the 20's advanced until the famous, or infamous, plus-fours had reached a size when it was almost difficult to walk comfortably. These monstrous breeches competed with the plunder-hose of the sixteenth century, hanging full and baggy over the brightly-coloured, hand-knitted stockings to within a few inches of the ankle (Fig. 152 A). Ornamental knitted garters with fringed ends showed beneath the breeches, and brogues – with a leather flap, punched and decorated as well as fringed – were normally worn. A cloth cap with a large peak and clipped down crown, often made of the same tweed as the suit, completed this particular outfit.

Within a few years of this vogue, plus-fours were no longer singled out for the golfer. They had become the casual costume for almost any daytime need and from 1926 onwards were worn as much in towns as the countryside and on the beach.

At about the same time Oxford trousers or 'Bags', as they were then called, made their first appearance (Fig. 152 B). In light pastel shades of grey or brown, pinky-beige, blue-grey or Lovat these ungainly trousers flapped through the dance halls and *thé dansants*

Fig. 152. – 1927

'Charlestoning' and 'Black Bottoming' with their lithe companions in beaded dresses.

It was correct to wear a darker coat with these trousers which could be either double-breasted or cut with long lapels.

This was a period of dress reform for men, and new experiments in sports clothes introduced such garments as the short-sleeved sports shirt, shorts for tennis and 'hiking', coloured shirts with collars attached, dressing gowns for beach wear and a host of play clothes which really gave more freedom from restriction than had previously been known.

Tailoring tended towards padded shoulders and chest with a slightly emphasized waist; dinner jackets and, occasionally, evening dress suits were made in some subtly dark shade that might pass for black – midnight blue, charcoal or even very dark claret. The tails of dress suits were longer and the cut-away front shorter so that the waistcoat showed some inches beneath. Sometimes a cummerbund was worn in place of the waistcoat. Most of these styles were to be seen around 1930.

In summer, shoes, made of white buckskin and trimmed with black or brown leather, were much worn. They were, however, vulgarly referred to as 'co-respondent shoes' and not considered quite 'the thing'.

Amongst the clothes that could be seen about the house or even at the seaside were included the lounge dressing gown and Russian pyjamas. The dressing gown was donned over evening trousers and often worn with an elegant silk scarf at the throat so that the stiff collar could be removed. Such garments were made from silk or satin and carried gorgeous designs of dragons or some brilliant pattern. The lapels were often quilted or made from some plain material such as velvet or satin. They were worn by the host at an informal gathering and played a great part in the theatre of the time which rather specialized in intimate domestic scenes.

The main contrast between the 20's and the 30's lay in the fact that the dress reform was accepted in the 30's and no longer considered strange and outrageous; the extremes in width of trousers and breeches had become old-fashioned and the idea of colour was accepted as a masculine privilege as well as a feminine one.

There is actually little of note in the tailoring of the 30's once the styles had settled into place, though materials and colours changed considerably. It is possible to study a pile of photographs and tailors' plates between the years 1930 and 1950 and find practically no obvious difference in the cut of a lounge suit or dinner jacket. Possibly to the tailor himself they may have had slight important details to be observed each year but such things are not noticeable in a general comparison. There is perhaps a slight padded look above the waist in the early 30's and the waist itself may appear a trifle higher in the fashion plates but from a photograph these details are not visible.

With greatcoats there is a difference; the introduction of a Teddy-Bear coat (Fig. 155 A) with a belt was typical of the 30's. The wind-cheater and the lumber jacket both made their first appearance in this country.

Colour schemes, once so formal, began to go gay and wild. This was possibly due to the then Prince of Wales' choice of colour. A photograph of 1930 shows him wearing a peach-coloured shirt, pink tie striped in red and blue, a yellow pull-over with red and blue lines round the V neck, a brown checked tweed jacket and an orange handkerchief in the breast pocket.

In 1936 a gentleman's evening cloak was described as follows: 'Cut in midnight blue cloth, the cloak is lined with white satin buttoned to the inside with buttons hidden in the folds.' And, in the same year, the *Tailor and Cutter* informs us that 'at a social function in the West End clothes were intriguing. Impeccable morning coats . . . a blue worsted suit, black waistcoat with white spots, pale blue shirt, white collar and check tie, brown suit with cream shirt and double collar and old gold handkerchief.'

Tweed suits showed variety in colour; the Harris tweed of a few years earlier, with its large checked patterns, was replaced by smaller designs, no less colourful but with a tendency towards a general heather mixture tone rather than the contrasts of the last decade. Fair Isle pull-overs with exaggerated plus-fours were still to be seen on the golf course but a particular interest in plain coloured pull-overs was more personal.

For a decade there had been no emphasis on the female waist-line. In fact, clothes were designed to show off the slenderness of youth unrestricted, but the growing interest in longer dresses demanded that some sort of emphasis on curves might once again be obtained from a fitted waist or even a belt — no longer on the hips but at the waist. By 1931 the day dresses were longer, fuller and some 5 or 6 inches below the knee (Fig. 153 B); evening and formal dresses were down to the ground. Long dresses were worn for any special occasion and, once again, the 'picture frock' with a small emphasized waist and bouffant skirts made its appearance (Fig. 153 A). However, the most popular long dress was one cut with swirling skirts whose fullness flared out from the knees rather than the waist. Such skirts were often a complete circle of material attached cleverly to the gown which was itself cut on the cross (Fig. 154 A).

Hats, also, returned to the 'picture' quality, large and floppy for

A   B

Fig. 153. – 1930

summer garden parties or weddings but folded back off the face and dragged down over the ears for normal wear, the felt being pinned with some sort of diamanté ornament at side or front.

There was a special emphasis on the shoulders of practically all dresses during the early 30's which, later in the decade, developed into a definite widening and padding, leg-of-mutton and even heavy gathering at the shoulder.

The emphasis in the early 30's was achieved by frills at the shoulders, circular or half circle sleeves fitting at the armhole and

Fig. 154. – 1934

falling in layers to the elbow; or a tiny shoulder-cape, epaulettes or some sort of draped collar always cut to flare. The ingenuity of the really good dressmakers of the time was an experiment of flared draperies, tucks and pin-tucks and a desire that the dress should not be either simple to make or easy to copy.

By about 1935 tight waists, wide shoulders and fairly straight skirts, with perhaps a slit at the side for comfort because they were long (7 inches from the ankle), and a much smaller hat had altered the fashionable silhouette considerably (Fig. 155 B).

The flares of the first five years were already a thing of the past and the boning of evening gowns became a necessity because they were now worn without any sort of shoulder strap. Boned from breast to hip they gave an hour-glass contour above the immensely full, ankle-length skirts. Hair, which had been gradually getting longer, was worn in a variety of styles, no longer a uniform head but

Fig. 155 – 1937

sometimes cut in a pageboy shoulder-length cut, sometimes worn curling on the shoulders, sometimes done up on the top of the head with a bunch of curls.

The whole trend in dress turned towards something essentially feminine and even vaguely Victorian for formal wear. The leg-of-mutton sleeves, puffed shoulders and full skirts (for evening) emphasized the waist in comparison although no actual tight lacing took place (Fig. 156 B). Frilly petticoats peeked out coyly under these billowing skirts and by 1938, when skirts were beginning to get shorter again, little frills of white lace appeared under the day dresses (Fig. 156 A). The correct way to wear such frills was under a dark dress so that the full benefit of contrast could be seen.

Many of the summer dresses of 1939 were made with a frill of lace sewn under the hem to imitate a petticoat.

The main difference between the short skirts of the 20's and those of the late 30's lay in the fact that those of the 30's were full and swung from the waist displaying extremely elegant sheer silk stockings of various natural coloured hues. Those of the 20's were hung from the shoulders and hips and the stockings were not natural tones and neither were they particularly elegant. Pinky-beige and just pink artificial silk and lisle were more often worn than real silk because, at that time, experiment in finely woven stretchy materials had not really progressed at the rate required by such a sudden exposure of limbs previously covered decorously by long skirts.

The Second World War put a stop to any further experiment in fashions and the clothes rationing, almost throughout the 40's, made every new garment a problem and a new outfit impossible. Utility fashions were designed strictly for economy in material and the man who was not in uniform found that his socks barely covered the ankle, that he had no waistcoat to his suit, no pyjamas, no tails to his shirt and no turn-ups to his trousers. Women's dresses, already short, remained at knee level, skimpy and with inadequate seams.

With extraordinary persistence, in spite of the almost insuperable difficulties of finding a hairdresser, their hair remained long and curled, puffed and piled up on top of the head or hanging loose on the shoulders. Perhaps one of the more noticeable fashions of the first few years of the War was the Mozart coiffure or the Pompadour head. Hats, the only unrationed article of clothing, continued to be jaunty and sophisticated. Otherwise, apart from a vast quantity of new uniforms, fashions remained unchanged.

Dior's 'New Look' in 1947, with his breathtaking extravagance in

A   B

Fig. 156. – 1939

fabrics, startled the war-weary into a new appreciation of feminine fashions. Full ballet-length dresses with neatly fitting tops, large picture hats and, once again, the swathed dress with a skirt some 7 inches from the ground and a tightly-fitting top with an hour-glass insistence on both waist and hips, quickly took the fancy of those whose life had been restricted to uniforms for the past five or six years. The appeal of the longer dress was so great that even rationing did not prevent the 'New Look' from its almost immediate success (Fig. 157 A).

In 1948 hair was once again cut short. This time it was the 'Urchin' cut and, following the line of the head, slightly tousled, it was not a great deal different from the Eton crop of the 20's though this time it was allowed to curl and not stuck to the head.

From *Country Life* of 1950 we learn that the 'straight skirt is usual . . . livened by detail of cut. Inverted pleats and godets are hidden away, from the knee level down, on many of the country suits. Jackets fasten high on the chest, nip the waist and are slightly stiffened about the basques. Pockets on basques bell out either side enough to be noticeable . . . the coat is cut with raglan sleeves and a slim sloping shoulder line that creates a pyramid silhouette.'

Here we have the latest country fashions and their descriptions tally with Fig. 157 c.

High collars and sloping shoulders, waisted suits with a slightly flared basque, draped off the shoulder afternoon and evening dresses were typical of the early 50's.

Dior had created a longer skirt and the majority continued to follow the master until about 1957 when skirts began to rise again towards the knees, and stiletto heels began to leave their mark in stately homes, museums and aeroplanes before those who cared for the beauty of their floors had realized what damage this new fashion could accomplish in a very short space of time.

During the 50's some of the most extraordinary experiments in young men's clothes began. A slightly exaggerated cut in men's suits had taken place almost as soon as clothes rationing had ceased. This was supposed to recapture something of Edwardian splendour with a high buttoned coat and tighter-fitting trousers; the trend was caught and exaggerated by those catering for the young man who had just begun to earn a salary and 'Teddy Boy' suits took the young Londoner by storm. Almost simultaneously the 'Zoot Suit' arrived. This was supposedly inspired by the clothes worn in films by Chicago toughs and consisted of a long, almost

Fig. 157. — 1950

knee-length jacket with a velvet collar and huge pockets. Neither of these fashions remained in favour for long as a new freedom for youth had been heralded from a student community who were beginning to make an impression with their 'casual' clothes.

Throughout the Teddy Boy period long-toed shoes, commonly referred to as winklepickers, were worn and for a few years it was extremely difficult for anyone to find shoes without pointed toes.

Within a year of the freedom from utility cut clothes (1949), fashion demanded an apparently reckless abundance of material; even coats were full skirted with deep pleats or wide flares. They were often double breasted and carried wide, deep pockets. Many of these were reversible in thick blanket cloth or lively tweeds. Three-quarter-length flared coats, as wide as capes, floated out and away from the long, tightly-fitting skirts (Fig. 158). Suede waistcoats and jerkins made their appearance and afternoon and evening dresses with full, stiff petticoats springing out from a waist which was now

Fig. 158. – 1953

retained by a boned undergarment known as a 'Waspie'. Such dresses were normally some 6 or 8 inches from the ankle and many of the newest day dresses were hardly shorter.

Beach clothes and those termed 'Bright new play clothes' made a very effective appeal to practically everyone. Jeans, Bermudas, shorts and various extravagances in American cowboy shirts and lacy little off-the-shoulder blouses (that tied under the breasts and left a midriff free to the sun) could be found on any beach or wherever there might be a little sunshine and warmth.

Such garments were indeed the forerunners of various plunging necklines and experiment in revealing various parts of the anatomy became a new trend for fashion designers.

In 1953 a new interest in hats produced a variety from 'Coolie' to 'Pillbox' and these were acclaimed as the 'prettiest hats for years'. Many of these were made on a minute frame that fitted across the head from ear to ear.

Fig. 159. — 1958

In the same year we can also see that the fashion houses were making a colossal effort to introduce new styles in coats. Dior showed a 'dome-shaped half-length coat', Givenchy a two-third-length 'tapering coat'; Balenciaga a three-quarter-length coat that went in at the bottom and Fath a seven-eighths 'flared redingote'.

1954 and 1955 saw the beginning of Dior's new themes on letter shapes – first the H line, then the A and Y, each letter indicating where the emphasis was to be – either on a wide shoulder, a wide hem or a straight and narrow skirt. By the time these particular ideas had filtered into the English shops they had been slightly altered and the Y had become something of a favourite because the majority of English women were more aware of their slim hips and long legs than were their sisters across the Channel (Fig. 159).

By 1957 the skirt length was generally at the knee again. A high waist gave a certain length to the skirt but the 'sack', the 'trapeze' and the 'sheath' dress all had their followers. The 'trapeze' shape was used extensively for coats. These were supremely full and swung

Fig. 160. – 1960

in majestic folds from neck to hem. The 'sheath' or 'sack', being without any waist-line, was much the same as the dresses of the mid-1920's.

This was the first year of 'shortie' nightclothes and a host of new sports items as well as the stiletto heel and narrowing pointed-toed shoe.

Nothing particularly remarkable except variations on the same themes and a fascinating series of experiments in hose and tights marked the passing of the years until 1965 when the 'Mini Skirt' or 'Minuscule' as it was first called, created some considerable disturbance. In its early days the skirt was a skirt only, and not a dress, of extreme brevity worn with gaily patterned hose or tights in a variety of designs from gaudy floral to thick knits of fascinating textures and unusual colours. Some skirts were worn over a sweater made from the same material as the hose which gave an amusing effect of coloured rehearsal 'leotards' and tights, with a brief skirt worn over them (Fig. 161). At about this time the long-toed shoes with their stiletto heels were discarded in favour of something less

Fig. 161. — 1965

elegant and more in keeping with the boyish look of the mini-skirted young. Shoes with an ankle strap and low, square heel, ankle boots and square-toed shoes of shiny coloured plastics, numerous rather ugly and clumsy shoes were fashion's choice. Knee and above the knee boots were increasingly popular from 1966 onwards. Long, straight hair hanging from a centre parting or having a heavy fringe added to the extremely youthful effect of such fashions. At the same time, however, all the fashion magazines still showed how much the knee-length dress was worn and how few were the followers of the mini-skirted craze.

Wigs and hairpieces played a great part in the hairdressing of a more sophisticated community. The 'Caftan' and long straight skirt replaced the minis after dark.

By 1967 the mini had taken over – almost to the exclusion of a longer dress, and a variety of fun-furs, not necessarily made to resemble fur, helped the young to be up to date without spending a great deal of money in doing so. The 60's, even more than the 50's, catered, in all respects, for youth. In 1968 the maxi-coat made its appearance worn with a mini-skirt and high boots (Fig. 162 A).

Hard-wearing leather jerkins, coats, breeches, suits etc. were replaced by garments made from synthetics, which gave much the same effect with less costly outlay.

The 'Wet Look' of plastics was generally a much advertised and equally well patronized method of making their sale even quicker and more profitable.

Almost identical suits in black leather or imitation leather, heavily studded with brass, were worn by both sexes and were, however, almost exclusive to the teenagers, replacing their hipster jeans and T-shirts of the summer months.

Student fashions had broken away completely from the normal run of clothes and had established fashions of their own, which included almost anything that looked slightly grotesque or capable of shocking a more conventional generation. This was a craze that sent students to junk shops and jumble sales in search of peculiar wardrobes and eventually materialized in the Carnaby Street and King's Road shops, starting a new trade designed exclusively to fill this need for 'way out' clothes.

The same spirit of change affected the hairdressing for men. The long-haired, bearded and heavily-moustached student, who preferred not to waste his energies and money on shaving or going to a hairdresser soon became the leader of the fashion and by the close

A   B

Fig. 162. – 1969

of the 60's long hair of almost any length became an accepted style, much as it had done during the reign of Charles I.

It was also during the 60's that a real breakaway from traditional tailoring managed to shoulder its way into polite society (Fig. 162 B).

Shirts with polo necks and no ties made their appearance, shirts with frilled fronts and jabots, shirts made from Indian saris, shirts of gay floral prints, plain coloured shirts of every conceivable colour with frills at the wrist and wide cravats or falling bows filled the shop windows and graced every gay occasion. Brightly-coloured suits in previously unheard-of colours for men were no longer re-markable and the velvet suit or elegantly cut trousers in velvet, tightly fitting from hip to knee and flaring slightly from knee to instep once more made the young man into something of a dandy on the occasions when he wanted to look elegant. This was a decade that permitted individuality in the choice of colour and dress for men almost for the first time since Regency days, 150 years earlier.

INDEX